Black Boy

The Wounded Healer

To: Mike

From:
Dr. Frederick Bro

keep learning about
yourself

By

Dr. Frederick Dare Brockington

Table of Contents

Dedication

This book is dedicated to mother Mamie Ruth Brockington and my Father Richard Brockington and all 13 of my siblings, and nieces, and my nephews and friends.

I'm grateful for all the love you have given me!

Acknowledgment

Many people have helped write this book a reality. I would like to thank my family. I love you all, and I am nothing without you. The experiences I have had with you made me who I am today. I would like to thank my friends who constantly kept checking on the book's status to ensure I was on task with completing it. I thank all the people who read the book in its draft form to help me make the book better. Last but not least, I would like to thank myself for being brave enough to share my story with the world in order for it to help the world.

About the Author

Frederick Dare Brockington, PhD, is a national certified Counselor, Associate Licensed Therapist, Singer, Songwriter, and Zumba Instructor. Dr. Brockington currently works in a private practice with clients who are experiencing anxiety. He has a Master's in Clinical Mental Health Counselling, and a PhD in Advanced Studies of Human Behavior Counselling. Dr. Fred, as his clients call him, is originally from Hampton, Virgina, but currently resides in Atlanta, Georgia. Dr. Fred is the youngest of 13 children. He loves his family and thanks his parents for instilling in him a love for his family, and a great work ethic.

Black Boy Anxiety

Hey Black boy, hey Black girl, it's okay to have trauma

We do not have a choice of living without it

Trauma does not know color or gender

It hides inside your brain, waiting to start trouble

Black boy and Black girl when trauma is ready

It will come back later to start more trouble

Trauma calls its friends anxiety

When you least expect it, Anxiety will get you

But don't be afraid to discuss it

Anxiety can be handled if you just acknowledge it

(Dr. Frederick Dare Brockington)

Introduction

I am an African American male, a mental health therapist, and I experienced burn trauma, verbal abuse, the loss of loved ones, and other traumatic experiences early in life. This book explains how traumatic experiences impacted my mental health and the journey I traveled to achieve better mental health. I wrote this book because I struggled with understanding what mental health looks like, and I finally figured out that my life had been damaged by anxiety, which could have been treated many years ago if treated timely.

As an African American male, I also explore how the African American community has a perspective about mental health illness, and I explain mental health terminology that may seem foreign to brown and black communities. My goal is to help minorities understand that mental health treatment is just as important as physical health.

This book starts with my personal story of what I believed triggered my mental health illness and a description of what mental health is. I then continued to explore what mental health is and what was happening to me.

To anyone who can relate to me at any point while reading a book, I want you to know that whatever you are feeling and going through right now will be over if and only if you decide to cater to it timely.

Chapter 1: My Life Story

The burn, a traumatic experience; in 1972, I lived at 332 Catalpa Ave, Hampton, VA 23661 with my family. I was the baby of 13 children by the same mother and father. My mother and father had me later in life, so some of my older siblings were out of the house living their own lives. There were ten rooms in the two-story white house with a large front porch and a nice large backyard. My mom and dad had their own room. The rest of my brothers and sisters, including me, shared bedrooms. I was two years old at the time. On one Tuesday afternoon, my sister had bathed me, and I was getting dressed for the day. She helped me put on my shorts and t-shirt.

I was always looking for things to play with throughout the house.

I started playing with the small green military men who were in my toy box in the corner of my bedroom. I pretended the toy figures were fighting against each other in a make-believe war. This playtime lasted for about 30 minutes, then boredom set in. I dropped the military toy figures in the middle of the floor and moved on to my next adventure. I noticed my view master in the corner of the living room, and I picked it up to see a 3D vision of my favorite cartoon character. I dropped the view master down on the floor, and

I decided to see what would pique my interest in the rest of the house.

We had a big kitchen attached to the dining room area. I loved being in the kitchen because this is where my family always gathered for Sunday dinner. Those dinners were fun and exciting. So, I walked my way to the kitchen. My sister yelled from the bedroom, "Do not go into the kitchen," but as I was bored, I decided to explore, so I entered the room anyway. Also, I never listened to my siblings when they would tell me to do something. When I entered the kitchen, I saw the big white stove that had a pot of something boiling. I saw the steam vapors float up to the top of the ceiling from afar. I could not see what was in the pot because I was not tall enough to get a full view. I remember getting frustrated, wondering what was in the cooking pot because it always smelled so good. I loved when my mother used to make chicken gravy and white rice.

My mind wandered over to the kitchen corner, where I noticed a mop that seemed very fascinating. It had a long, bright yellow handle with a white cloth mop head. I grabbed it and imagined it was a train to ride. I put my right leg across the mop stick and pretended I was traveling across the country on a make-believe train ride. I was riding the train to see my grandparents in South Carolina. Before I knew it, I bumped into the big white stove, and the top of the mop hit the pot's handle. I let out the loudest scream! Tears were streaming down my face! I was jumping all around the kitchen, hoping the pain would stop. I could see my skin melting off of me. I was petrified. The boiling water cascaded over my head, chest, and arms. I let out the most horrible scream, and on hearing my painful cry, my older brothers and sisters came running from the other rooms of the house to see what had happened. There I was, in the middle of the kitchen floor, burned from hot scalding water. The pain felt like someone had poured green rubbing alcohol on an open wound. I was in complete shock. My brothers and sisters were screaming and crying hysterically. I was rushed to the hospital immediately!

Healing:

Once I made it to the local hospital, the doctors knew I needed extensive burn treatment. I was transferred by helicopter to a neighboring hospital that was specialized in burn trauma. The doctors told my parents that the treatment involved a skin graft from my thigh to the severely burned areas. I was admitted to the hospital for several months. I remember feeling lonely and afraid at the hospital. The doctors and the nurses would come in and out of the room to provide me with treatment. The nurses would talk to me and assure me everything would be okay. They tried to offer me motherly care, but nothing would work. I just wanted to be in my mother's arms, but this could not happen because I was severely burned. I could not touch certain parts of my body until I was fully healed. It was hard for me not to touch my body! I still felt the pain! My parents visited the hospital every day, but my mother could not hold or comfort me because of the severe burns all over my body. I missed my family; I wanted to go back to playing at home.

Finally, I was released from the hospital once my burns began to heal. For the next few months, I had to follow up on doctor's appointments. My family members had to take special care of me. They had to learn how to bathe me and look after me. I had to deal with the new me. How long it took to recover from this ordeal entirely is all a blur for me. During that time, my intermittent memory loss was probably the coping mechanism that helped me avoid the pain of this experience.

Family guilt:

My mother felt like everyone in the neighborhood and the church would blame her for the accident. I didn't find this information out until later in life when I overheard my mother talking about my burn trauma with my aunt. I think she thought I held her responsible for what happened to me, but I didn't. I thought it was an accident I had caused. My mother and father went through sadness due to this experience. My sisters and brothers also suffered guilt that I would not have gotten burned if they had paid more attention. In our household, there was not one sibling who was solely responsible for me; it was a team effort because they were all so genuinely worried about me. As a child, my parents did not take me to psychotherapy after my burn. I do not blame my parents for this because they probably were not aware that this event would impact my life so greatly; this is the thing with trauma, you never know what event triggers your mental health. They were just so happy that their son survived such a horrific accident. After I came home from the hospital, my mother stood up in front of the church congregation to testify that God had saved my life. She stated that God had a plan for my life, and I would help others one day. Also, my parents were older, so therapy was never mentioned in their parents' homes either. The pastor of the church prayed for our family and me during this grief period. Eventually, the guilt and the shame of the situation decreased.

Avoidance:

I really do not know which member of the family put the boiling water on the stove. I do not know precisely who was babysitting me at the time, but it was usually a family effort. My family and I never discussed that detail. My family never discussed problems in detail. We just waited for the issue to be resolved or disappear on its own; we used to deal with it in denial. The secrecy of this disturbance is how most black families handle situations like this. Stop talking about it and move on with your life, which was exactly what we did. Note to parents of black children or any child: If something like this happens to your child, therapy needs to be provided to you and your child. As I write, tears come to my eyes because I survived this traumatic event, and I realized how much the burn experience impacted my life and how much I needed therapy at that time. The sad part is, I didn't even know I was in dire need of it.

My life changed:

Children adjusting to a burn trauma can experience various psychological issues pertaining to adjusting to their new persona

1. This burn experience was a lot of pressure for me to bear. As an adult, I am slowly figuring out that I experienced body image issues, stress, anxiety, and low self-esteem growing up. Childhood burn is one of the most traumatic injuries a child could experience and could create additional stressors in the child's social life

2. I survived the physical injury, but mentally, this tragedy is with me for the rest of my life. I have scars on my chest, neck, and on my left arm near my hand. The burns are deep and extend from the rest of my dark smooth

skin. Some of them are very noticeable, and some of the burns require you to really stare at me to see them.

Telling my life story to my elementary school classmates:

I attended Wythe Elementary School from kindergarten through sixth grade. Wythe Elementary was a three-story building nestled in the Wythe area of Hampton, Virginia. It was down the street from my family home, so I walked to school every day. My friends in the neighborhood were also my classmates. The student population was very diverse, and I felt very at home.

As a child, I accepted the scars and lived life as normal as I could. In elementary school, my classmates would ask what happened to me, and I would tell my story as much as I could remember. It was hard narrating from scratch to each one of them. During playtime, I would sometimes notice the facial expression of classmates change when they spotted the burns. During this time, that did not bother me. At this young age, it was all about playtime with my friends. I would always tell friends and classmates that my burns would go away when I got older if they asked. I have no idea where that statement came from, but I remember using it often after telling my story. My narrative about my burn was a way for me to take the attention away from the burn and focus on the future me.

Hiding the scars:

As I got older, I started becoming more self-conscious about my scars. In my first year of middle school, I was enrolled in a physical fitness class (PE). For this class, I had to change from my regular school clothes into a t-shirt and shorts. I had so much anxiety about changing clothes in the locker room in front of my classmates.

One day, I was changing in the locker room, and Peter, a neighborhood friend, and classmate saw my burn marks. "Oh my God," he yelled! "What happened to you?" Everyone in the locker room stared at me as if I had committed a crime. I felt humiliated, and after that day, I found a shower stall where I would change clothes for classes. I never wanted to be looked at like that again. After coping with this situation, my anxiety did calm down, but this was a rough time in my life. I didn't think about talking with the PE teacher to see if I could change into my gym clothes privately. I didn't think young children like me had the right to voice concerns or issues, and I was taught to obey my elders.

Coping skills:

Children develop coping skills to handle adverse events; well, I coped with my burn scars by covering myself up with long sleeves and collared shirts to avoid attention. The scars on my chest could be covered up by wearing a shirt, and my arms could be covered up with a long sleeve shirt, even in the summer sometimes. My neck, which has a huge scar, could be covered up using a collared shirt. I was always afraid that people would judge me due to my scars or that I would get strange looks once they noticed them.

If I went to the beach, I would wear a tank top that would cover most of my scars. I never went to the beach shirtless. If I got into a pool and many people were around, I would always wear a shirt in the pool. I had low self-esteem because of this, but I made the best of it. My family taught me that if you work hard, and you can achieve anything you want. I thought that if I didn't let it distract me from my life, I would be fine.

Childhood anxiety:

Looking back at this experience, I felt shame, anxiety, and fear of being criticized. One day, I was the first person in the school lunch line, which was good because no one was directly behind me for about five minutes. I could smell the hamburgers being grilled, and my school had the best french fries. Suddenly, the lunch line was long, and there were about ten students behind me. I began to panic. I didn't like anyone behind me for a long time because eventually, they would see my scars. I became very anxious and fidgety until I was out of the line.

On one occasion, my classmate Lisa was behind me in the lunch line, and she started touching my scar. I got agitated and told her to stop before I hit her. This type of situation happened to me almost daily. My burn experience is one of the triggers that started my anxiety. Mothers of burned pre-school children reported their children having behaviors such as anxiety and increased temper tantrums. My burn trauma produced my anxiety at this stage of my life.

Childhood trauma:

It is essential to explore childhood trauma because if the bad experience is not processed, it can lead to mental health issues later in life. After the burn event, I seemed okay, but my life changed once I started growing up. Traumatic events increase the risk for post-traumatic stress disorder (PTSD), major depressive disorder (MDD), and generalized anxiety disorder (GAD) (3). Since I didn't process my negative experiences at an early age, I suffered from many anxieties related to my burn, but I continued to move on with my life.

Processing means to sit with your emotions, understand the feelings, and figure out how the incident has impacted your life. Processing trauma allows the individual to explore the feelings and emotions they experienced during the adverse life event and identify the coping skills they used to cope with the dire situation.

The verbal abuse – a traumatic experience:

In 1978, it was a hot summer day on Catalpa Ave in Hampton, Virginia. Most of the families on our block knew each other. Many of them had a child out in the neighborhood, either at the local school playground, fishing at the Chesapeake Bay, riding a bike, sitting on the front porch, hanging out with friends, or getting ice cream from High's Ice Cream store. I knew almost everyone in the neighborhood. I would often be recognized as one of the Brockington kids. I had an active family. My brothers loved to play basketball, and my sisters were cheerleaders for our local school. If I got into some trouble, my parents would know about it before I even made it home. The neighborhood was safe for the most part. There were a lot of trees and streetlights on every corner. My friends and I would play kickball at the empty corner lot. On Friday afternoons, a group of boys and girls played an intense game of kickball, which was always fun. It was kind of a ritual. Once the streetlights came on, all of us headed back to our homes.

Name-calling:

As my friends and I made our way home, we walked through the now almost dark Catalpa Avenue. We quickly approached a group of older teenagers. I immediately recognized all of them because they were my brother's friends. I got nervous and wanted to take a different route home because I saw my brother, and he was drinking. As early as I could remember, my brother Roy was always drinking beer and smoking cigarettes. He would constantly call me names and bully me for no reason. I knew Roy would start some crap, and I didn't have the mental capacity to deal with it. Roy tended to bully my other siblings and me in the past. "Get home, you punk!" he shouted. "Why are you always hanging with a bunch of girls?!" I felt embarrassed and wanted to get into the house as fast as I could. I would, of course, tell him to shut up, but that would only make the situation worse. Roy would make sure he got the last word, and I felt worse. So, I learned just not to respond.

There was another time that I remember playing in front of my house with my friends. Roy was in the yard talking, drinking, and smoking with his friends. Suddenly, he started calling me names like faggot, punk, and many other derogatory terms. These names really hurt because he accused me of being gay, and I was just myself. His friends laughed at me, and my friends laughed as well. I felt so bad and anxious that I wanted to run and hide. This happened countless times, and that is why I really did not like my brother.

Avoidance of embarrassment:

My feelings of fear and anxiety would increase every time he was around. I am not sure if his behavior impacted any other family members as it affected me because of my burn trauma. I always thought I was being extra sensitive, so I started avoiding him. I was already dealing with the past negative life event. After each argument, my family and I would not discuss the situation that had happened the night before. We would continue with life like nothing ever happened.

My coping mechanism was to be quiet and avoid my brother when he was drinking, not to embarrass me in front of my friends or make me feel very sad. I was approximately five or six years old trying to handle this situation. When my brother was not drinking, he did not communicate a lot. I avoided and hated him at the same time. When I would see him outside the house with his friends, I would avoid him like the plague.

Arguments in the middle of the night:

One night, I was sound asleep in my room next door to Roy's room. Suddenly, the rest of the family and I were awakened around midnight by a loud argument. My brother Roy was arguing with my middle brother. Roy, who was about 18 years old at the time, was very angry for some reason. It seemed like every other day, Roy would drink, and he would start an argument with one of our family members. He would usually agitate everyone about the minor things. Roy accused my 15-year-old brother of wearing his brand-new pants. They were getting louder and louder. The arguments were usually were resolved by the police. The police would typically ask what the argument was about. My father would be the spokesperson for the family. My brother Roy would start arguing with the officers as well, but I cannot remember if he was ever arrested or not. I was afraid to touch anybody's stuff in the house for fear of being cursed out. I lived a life of nervousness when Roy was around.

Generational curse:

There was a rumor that my mother's brothers killed each other back in South Carolina. I overheard this rumor from my aunts when they came to visit one summer from South Carolina. I believed it only because I could see this scenario happening in my family with my brother, Roy. I thought my family had a generational curse that would surely end in my brothers killing each other. My mother was traumatized by the arguments because this was like history repeating itself. When Roy created chaos in the family, my mother would always remind her of her deceased brother. This argument scenario played out almost my entire childhood. Roy created an anxious environment in the home when he was around, but he also made an uneasy climate for me outside the home.

Anxious and scared to death:

I was so scared and anxious, and I thought my brothers were going to kill each other. My anxiety was high. Every night, I feared an argument would break out, so I was always worried. I would cover my head with a blanket, hoping this would stop very soon. I could hear my dad yelling at them to be quiet and go to sleep, but they kept it going, and then they started physically fighting. My sisters and I were crying, not sure of the situation's outcome, and it intensified. My mother would cry hysterically, asking them to please stop. My mother was not in good health, and I always felt like these arguments made her health worse.

Family anxiety:

I felt anxious when the verbal abuse and the arguments would happen. The feelings of nervousness, fear, sadness and worry were my normal feelings as a child. I look back on this situation and wonder if my parents had anxiety over this? I am sure they were afraid of the outcome of this situation, but they were reticent about their feelings. Parental anxiety disorders increase the risk of children developing anxiety disorders. My parents were reticent and only spoke about things when they felt they needed to speak. My entire family experienced this anxiety, but our coping mechanism was avoidance. We would go to church on Sunday, and my mother would always cry out to God to help our family.

Sunday morning church tradition - another traumatic experience:

Every Sunday, my mom would cook a great breakfast and dinner. For breakfast, we would have grits, eggs, sausage, and buttered toast. For dinner, it was always a protein and rice with gravy and one of her famous desserts. In the morning, my siblings and I would take turns showering and getting dressed. Everyone would be dressed in their Sunday Best. We would arrive at church around 9:30 am. The church was a family tradition and my escape from the verbally abusive brother at home. Roy did not attend church. Most of my family attended the same church, a very small black church named the Church of Jesus. Our church members were like family. The church members would greet us at the door with big smiles. The pastor of the church was Dr. Merlin L. Ford. It was a Pentecostal church. I loved attending this church; it was where I established my relationship with God.

I was very active in the church. I attended Sunday school, I was an usher, and I sang in the choir. All of my family members had a role at the church at one time or another. My mother and sisters were bakers so that they would have bake sales for the church building fund. My father did not attend church, but he would drop us off and pick us up every Sunday. Some of my brothers would attend the church periodically. Most of us sang in the choir. I discovered my passion for music at this church.

I attended a choir rehearsal every week. The choir would travel to different churches within the community to sing. We were called the Church of Jesus Mass Choir, and we were well known in the community for our strong voices. Being in the choir is how my singing career started. I would lead songs, direct, and even "play" the organ for the choir. I was self-taught, and I enjoyed this experience in my younger days. All the church traditions made the church so much fun, but the church rules created anxiety for me.

Singing:

When I was younger, I could sing in front of anyone. I would sing for my family; I would sing for my classmates and friends. Singing was my coping mechanism to escape from the verbal abuse I received from my brother and the death of my loved ones. I have been a singer and songwriter since age five. I remember listening to gospel and rhythm and blues artists on the radio. I would learn all the lyrics to my favorite songs and sing the song as if I were on stage. When I listened to music, it made me emotional. Now, I think back on all the things I have been through; music makes me work out harder, and I can relieve the day's stress with a good sad song. I love sad songs the most because they allow me to release the tears of life, but listening to them does not make my face what is going on in my life.

Choir:

As I got older, I started singing with my church choir and participating in my school's local talent show. I was known in school as a singer and even participated in a singing group. I sang in the Hampton High School Acapella Choir as well as the Church of Jesus Mass choir. I was writing and recording music with my friends in a local music recording studio. I loved it! On Easter Sunday, the choir was in the reception hall of the Church of Jesus, waiting to sing in the service. We were all excited to perform the new song we had been rehearsing for weeks. I was going to lead the song. I was exceptionally nervous, but once I hit the stage, I was amazing. After the service, church members would congratulate me on how well of a solo performance I gave! Unfortunately, music was another way I avoided talking about a negative life event.

I would sit in front of the radio for hours listening to music. I would learn the lyrics and try to see how the song related to my life. Doing this helped me escape and avoid what problems were going on around me.

Fear of singing:

I signed up for a talent show in Downtown Atlanta. I had not performed in front of anyone in a long time, so I was excited and nervous at the same time. I had a few weeks to practice before the talent show. I practiced day and night until I felt I was ready to sing. I approached the stage, and my notes were flat, and I was trembling in FEAR! I could not face the audience. I sang with my eyes closed and got off the stage as quickly as possible. The problem is that the fear was not real. I was not afraid of anyone specific thing. I was afraid of the situation.

I began to fear what I loved most, which was singing in front of crowds. Before the anxiety took over, I would feel a little nervous at first, but after a few minutes, the anxiety would disappear. As I got older, as soon as I took the stage, I would sweat, and my body would shake profusely, and it was incredibly embarrassing. I remember being on stage. I was so nervous and sweating so much, I felt like the audience could feel my uneasiness. I started to avoid the thing I loved, so to continue my love for singing, I stayed away from the performing aspect, and instead, I began creating music videos to hear my music and my lyrics. Avoidance is how I resolved my social anxiety -- or so I thought.

Church Perfectionism, church rules, and being judged:

The church was my life! However, as a teenager, I began to feel like I had to be nearly perfect to be accepted at church, or I would be judged. My brother at home was already judging me. I didn't need more judges in my life. The church had its own set of problems. It had these rules that we all had to follow to be accepted in this environment. I struggled to live my life perfectly and tried to please my family and the church by doing the right thing as a Black teenage male. If I made a mistake, I could be blackballed from the church—all of this added unnecessary pressure.

Growing up in the church, I had to learn the rules of the church. Some of the regulations directly impacted my life, and some of them did not. Some examples of those rules were:

1. Women could not wear make-up, pants, or jewelry. My sisters would go shopping for very long dresses. They would spend hours in the store trying to find the perfect church outfit acceptable to the older church mothers. If my sisters wore a skirt that was above the knees, a church usher would quickly provide them with a blanket to cover their legs.

2. We were not allowed to play cards, go to the movies, or participate in anything secular. I never learned how to play cards because the church considered them the "devil's cards." My church friends could only attend movies that were rated PG-13 or had some biblically-based message. I could not listen to rhythm and blues music because it was not of God. The only type of music that was acceptable was gospel music.

3. Child out of wedlock, she could no longer participate in church activities. I remember being about seven years old when a teenage girl, who was a church member, got pregnant. She was asked to stand in front of the church and beg the church members for forgiveness. She was in tears, and all the members were staring at her in judgment. After that Sunday, the girl left the church. She was hurt and embarrassed. I felt terrible for her because it did not seem like she had any support to help her. According to church leadership, if you participated in any of these secular activities or engaged in pre-marital sex, you were going to hell. This let me know that if I were not perfect, I would be judged by church members, and I would surely be embarrassed.

4. You could not be a sinner! Being a sinner was defined as someone going against God's will. If you were a sinner, you had to be baptized and filled with the holy ghost. My goal during this time was not to be classified as a sinner.

Anxiety and church rules:

The rules controlled our behavior and created anxiety in myself and a lot of the congregation. I believe the church life I experienced was a blessing but damaging at the same time. I lived my life according to those rules, and when I could not fulfill all the requirements, I began to experience anxiety. I was trying to be perfect for the congregation and God. I

22

noticed many of my church friends had terrible relationships and got divorced; some then stopped going to church. The church environment I once loved became yet another environment I had to create a coping mechanism for, and it was avoidance. I avoided criticism, and I avoided feeling guilty for not fulfilling the church's requirements.

No one is perfect, but this environment made you feel like you had to be. There was a lot of judgment by the church. When I sang in front of the congregation, I had to have on the correct clothes. I could not be labeled a backslider, someone who was no longer connected to God and participated in worldly events.

Church members as judges:

I remember one Sunday morning, we were at the back of the church preparing to sing in the choir. We were all excited because we had practiced a new song. We all had on our purple and white choir robes. A close friend of mine and a church member was gay, and the entire church suspected it because of his feminine mannerisms. He had been seen by a church member the night before, hanging out at the local gay club. I had heard this before, but it did not matter to me. He was preparing to sing in the choir, and the church choir president approached him privately and told him he could no longer sing in the choir because he was gay. He told me what happened, and I apologized on behalf of the church. I felt

23

very upset that church members were so concerned about people's personal lives. I was disgusted! The church members were confined to being in this perfect box to fit in, and I felt like I lost myself trying to be perfect.

Church member's judgment:

Mother Thompson wore a loose yellow blouse and a long black skirt- she looked like a bumblebee. She sounded like a bumblebee when she gossiped to Sister Tayler about one of the church members being a lesbian. Mother Thompson said she saw the woman holding hands with another woman. "That type of behavior is not accepted in the church, and God is not pleased," stated Mother Thompson. This judgmental ideology was prevalent in the church. When backsliders returned to the church, they had to repent for their sins and wrongdoings before the church. I disagreed with this type of treatment. I felt embarrassed to belong to a church that treated people like this. It was as if the church was God over this individual's life.

There was this unspoken judgment against people who attended the church and did who did not follow the church's guidelines. I was tired of seeing this type of behavior. I was not perfect, and I didn't want my life to be put under a microscope by people who had their own skeletons in their closets. There were always rumors being spread about church members. I finally left the church due to the judgmental spirit that I think comes from the perfectionist mindset.

Social anxiety in the church:

I began to develop social anxiety. I was already feeling this from my brother's ridicule of me, and now I had the church judging my every move. No wonder I was afraid to be in a crowd or be the center of attention. Church trauma was another experience I didn't process, and now I will add death trauma to the already existing burn experience and the verbal abuse.

Chapter 2: Grief And Loss

Grief and Loss – a traumatic experience: Mom's death. Negative life events never stopped occurring. The older you get, the more likely it is that you will experience the death of a family member at some point. I was 25 years old at that time of my life. My best friend and I moved to Atlanta (ATL) in November 2001. The burn trauma, the verbal abuse, and the negative church experiences were all behind me physically, but mentally, they were still there lurking in the background.

Telling my mom, I was moving to Atlanta:

I had moved out of my family's home years ago and had a roommate. Before I moved to Atlanta, I visited my mother to tell her I was moving there. I pulled up to the family home, and I was very nervous because I knew she would be sad and worried. I would be the only child not living in Virginia with her. We had some small talk. I asked her how she was doing. We talked about church and the family. I finally gathered the courage and blurted out that I was moving. My mother was heartbroken, but I told her I would visit her often, and she did not have to worry about me.

Running from something:

I was running from something, but I didn't know what it was. I thought I would make a better life for myself in another state. I knew I had to relocate so I could grow as a young man. It was a tough transition, but it was a great decision. I found a great job and was moving forward in my life. There was hope that I could finally move on with my traumas. In 2005, I enrolled at Strayer University and graduated with my bachelor's in Business Administration a few years later.

My entire school life thus far in Atlanta was me avoiding past trauma. My burn experience and its impact on my body were always present in my mind. I talked to my family back home, but I was disconnected from them. I always felt that if I reached my educational goals, my life would be fantastic, and all the negative things I had experienced would be erased; boy! was I wrong. My goal was always to become successful so that I could help my family financially. My family was not poor, but I wanted more for them. I was going to be the one to make that happen, but I was broken. There was something that was constantly holding me back. Even though all the bad life events I had experienced were in the background, being avoided. As I pursued my academic goals, the family I was working so hard for somehow changed. I do not think I realized life could change so drastically. I was in denial. I couldn't understand what was wrong.

Mom in Virginia:

Meanwhile, in Virginia (2002), my mother was not feeling well and was rushed to the hospital. She was admitted, and the doctors were running tests.

"Hello, Fred," my sister said in a sad voice. I could feel the tears in her eyes.

"Hey, sis," I said with hesitation because my sister usually would not call me in the middle of a workday. I didn't know what she was about to say. "I called to let you know that Mom is not doing good. I don't think she is going to make it," she began to sob.

My heart dropped. I felt so heavy in my heart. Suddenly, I couldn't breathe. It was unbelievable. I didn't know what to do! I started searching for an airline ticket so that I could get on the next flight out. I was in panic mode, but before my travel plans were finalized, it happened. Later that day, my mother died, and I was never able to say goodbye. I couldn't make it, and it will always be one of the biggest regrets of my life.

The best mother ever:

My mom was the best. My mom had a different relationship with all 13 of her children, but she equally loved us. She always worked hard to help support her family. She taught us right from wrong. She did not play when it came to discipline. I remember getting a whipping when I did something wrong. "Fred, I told you

28

to clean your room!" I did with an attitude. "Who are you talking to like that?" My butt was sore from that whipping. After several of those whippings, I never acted out of line again.

She introduced us to God and religion. She always made sure we had a home-cooked meal. My mom could sew well. She would sew dresses for my sisters and herself. She always took time to sit and talk about God with me, my family, and friends. I went to many places with my mom, and I especially cherish our trips to the thrift store. These trips represented more than just a trip to the store. We spent quality time together during the car ride. Also, I would always find a used toy to play with while we were in the store, and mom always purchased it. My mom taught me the value of a dollar. You did not have to have new items to have a good time. She told me that there is a whole new level of peace when you stay in the shallowness of worldly things.

My mother was also the church's mother, so that we would have a lot of visits from the church ladies asking for advice and instruction on life situations. A raggedy Toyota pulled up to our house one Saturday morning. It was Sister Angela. She was there for her weekly prayer and conversation with Mother Brockington. I could hear Sister Angela crying out to the Lord and Mother Brockington crying and clapping in unison. My mother always made her guests feel at home whenever they visited. Everyone in the neighborhood knew my mother. The community respected her. Even though my mother struggled with past adverse life events and the current life situations, she was always positive. I think one of the reasons was that she had a strong connection, and she made herself spiritually strong.

Grieving my mother with avoidance:

I thought I had grieved about my mother's death, but I kept myself busy, so I would not think about it. I didn't want to believe that she was not with me anymore.

One Saturday morning, I put on my black suit and tie. Afterward, I helped my dad get dressed. All my brothers and sisters arrived at our family home sporadically. The entire family got into the funeral home's car to head to the funeral of our mother. In the car, we started sharing memories about Mom. But the environment in the car was sad and uncomfortable. We were trying to laugh but wanted to cry at the same time. We arrived at the Church of Jesus, which was only about 6 minutes away from our family home. The pews in the church were filled with church members, family, and friends. Front and center of the church lay my beautiful mother in her casket. Tears began to fall as I got closer to her. I sat down in the front pew. I was fixated on my mother so much that the entire service was a blur. At the end of the service, I kissed my mother's forehead and said goodbye.

This was the worst day of my life. My coping skills of avoidance were very well in place. I welcomed visitors to my family's house so that I would not have to face the sad feelings I had inside. I was devastated. After the funeral, I returned to Atlanta and continued to work and go to school, and before I knew it, the pain of my mother's death was in the background but still there. I coped with it by secretly crying. After all, one can never bear the pain of their mother. It is a difficult thing to move on, which needs time.

I had my moment of depression and anxiety, but I ignored it. My life was never the same after my mother died. It felt like the umbilical cord between my mother, and I was shattered. I was broken after this. My whole family was broken-hearted, but Mary did not get over my mother's death.

My sister's death:

Two years later, my sister Mary passed away. She was the oldest sibling in the family system. This was the second most horrible time in my life. My sister was only 54 years old. Mary and our mother were very close, and I genuinely think she died from a broken heart. They did everything together. They would spend hours on the phone talking about recipes, cooking, and clothes. But from a physician's perspective, she had a heart attack.

I loved my sister. She was married and out of our family home before I was born. She had three children, and we were all best friends. She lived about 10 minutes away from us, so she would come to visit her family often. I often visited her and played with my niece on Calhoun Street. I loved going to her house; it was my second home. She made our lives so much better. Mary had something special about her. She loved her family, and she let us know it. You could talk to her about anything. We would see Mary at church during the week. She would come over to visit on the weekends, and our family created so many beautiful memories. Amid our chaos, she was a calming spirit. Losing her was like losing an extended part of myself. I was going through so much pain that I thought I would die of a broken heart too.

Family traditions:

Mary, my mother, my sisters, my nieces, and I would go shopping on the weekends, and we would have a ball. On Easter weekend, we would shop for sewing patterns for my sister's and niece's outfits. They would take me to JC Penny's for my suit, or we would shop at multiple thrift stores looking for different items. I loved thrift stores because of this.

After the weekend shopping was over, we would meet at church the next day and enjoy Sunday dinner together afterward. We would enjoy Mary's baked goods because she was an incredible baker and cook. She could make anything you wanted. I don't think she used a lot of recipes either. I loved these moments more than anything. The joy of being around my family during this time was fantastic. If only I could revert time and cherish these moments once more.

This was our weekend tradition, so when she died, my heart broke again. I remember my entire family in tears as we laid her to rest. I remember seeing my dad crying, and that hurt me badly. I walked up to my sister's casket with my dad, and he broke down. I never saw my dad cry, and it triggered my tears even more. I never had a chance to say goodbye to my sister Mary, "Goodbye, sis! Rest in heaven."

Life was crazy after the death of my mom and my sister, but death did not stop because the following year, my nephew died.

Death

Death is brutal; we don't understand it.

We try to move on in life, but there is no handbook

Avoidance is Not the Key

I don't understand why

Death keeps coming after my family

By Dr. Frederick Dare Brockington

The murder of my nephew:

The last time I remember seeing Erik, my nephew, was at my sister's funeral. At that time, I didn't know this would be the last time I would see him. Erik had a girlfriend and a little girl. We did not keep up with each other as an uncle and nephew should, so I didn't know much about his life. I had moved to Atlanta when he was younger, and I didn't visit much initially. I knew he was a great person with much potential, but that potential was taken away from him and our family.

In 2005, three men drove into a driveway to meet an acquaintance about a drug deal. They were all seated in the front seat, so none of them would have to sit in the back with the stranger. The area was familiar, but the person they were meeting was not. "Something felt strange about the meeting," Erik said to himself, but he went along anyway. Parker came out of the house and approached the car. The driver began talking to Parker. He got into the backseat of the car. There was some exchange of products, but then Parker pulled out a gun and started shooting.

My nephew Erik was killed. Parker Rayford II was accused of gunning down three men, one of whom was my 23-year-old nephew. This was a drug deal gone wrong. I was devastated, as we were already in a bad place after losing my mom and sister. I could not deal with another tragedy. I later learned my nephew was trying to get away from being shot; it hurt my heart.

I was struggling:

I was depressed and losing weight and could not face my family. I avoided everything and everyone. I didn't allow anyone to know what I was going through. Life was tough. I was going out with friends and drinking a lot, trying to avoid how my life had turned out. I didn't expect to grow up to a life full of death and murder. My world was turned upside down once again. I regret that I didn't attend the funeral, but this was like a nightmare I was not ready to face. I felt like my brother resented me for not attending the funeral. Honestly, I didn't find out about my nephew's death until later. I never processed Erik's death. If I had attended the funeral, I would have had a chance to say goodbye and properly grieve. After this, life continued to knock me down.

My dad's death:

It was another blow. It was like the last nail in the coffin. My dad was my best friend. I would love to go to his bedroom, sit and watch TV, talk in between the shows, or just silently enjoy each other's company. We would watch wrestling shows. He was very supportive of anything I did in my life. He would always drop me off at my first job and pick me up. He listened to me often without saying a lot. My dad did not judge me. We went to several wrestling matches when I was a kid. All I remember is when my dad was excited about the fight; he would box as if he were one of the fighters. He never talked a lot, but his actions made me know that he loved me. He went to work every day and made sure his family was very well taken care of. I learned a lot about my work ethic from him. He would always be willing to lend a helping hand to anyone that needed it.

My dad worked for the City of Hampton. He was a supervisor, and a lot of people respected him. He would work long hours and would always make sure his family was okay. My dad had a drinking problem, but he did not let it prevent him from taking care of his family. I felt like my dad loved his family so much that even when he was drinking, his family came first.

One day, my mother walked into the living room with her white dress on, holding her purse in one hand and the Bible in the other. She was a quiet person, but her words were strong and passionate.

"Richard, are you coming to church this Sunday?" she asked.

He replied, "No, maybe next Sunday. But I will drop you off.]," my dad continued to watch television.

"Ok, you will need a relationship with God, and hopefully, one day, you will find God," my mother said in her calm and stern voice.

"I will!" he said in a sarcastic but calm voice. My dad got up, put on his clothes, and drove our family to church. My mother did not nag him or judge him. She loved my dad! Eventually, my dad gave up alcohol and started attending church faithfully. My dad was the best in the world.

Three years after my sister died, my father died. It seemed that death was a common thing at the time for my family. My dad was sick, so I often came home and visited him. I walked into the hospital room and saw my dad lying in his bed. He was smiling. His hair was a little grayer, but he was in good spirits. He was under the covers, and when he saw me, he sat up a little more. I said, "Hello, Dad," and he replied, "Hello!"

I asked him how he was doing, and he said, "I am okay. How are you doing?" he asked. "I am good, I came to see you," I told him.

"You need anything?" he asked.

"No! I came to see you."

"It is all about you." He said, and it melted my heart.

That is how my dad was. He looked out for his family no matter what. I told him I was here for him this time. My dad died while I was at the hospital. It was strange because he was talking to us for one minute and died a few minutes later. I was in disbelief. I never understood death and the way it worked. I now realize that death does not end the relationship. You keep the relationship going by exploring memories and remembering the lessons you were taught by the loved one. I retreated to my avoidance behavior by focusing on work and school. I had so much baggage at this time but did not realize I needed help. I was always to show my vulnerable side to anyone. It was hard for me to open up and share how I felt.

Life kept moving. I have had many deaths and bad things happen to my family and me over the years, so many that I cannot put them all in this book. I lost a sister-in-law and a brother-in-law. I have lost a lot of church friends to death. My life kept moving, and the trials and tribulations never stopped.

Stressed Out

The stress of life can bring you down

Negative life events will hang around

If you do not figure it out

Trauma will come back and stress you out

By Dr. Frederick Brockington

Chapter 3: Exploration Of My Mental Health

Whenever you are going through difficult times in life, the first thing that affects you is your mental health. As instinctive as it was, I neglected my mental health as well. At this point in my life, I was lost and living my life on autopilot. I was going with the flow and was totally numbed. I felt like an orphan. I continued to struggle with hiding the scars from anyone I met. I was afraid to be around men for fear that they would verbally abuse or judge me. My burn trauma and its impact on my body were always present in my mind. Some incidents never leave you alone and haunt you for the rest of your life; the same was the case with my bur trauma. If someone wronged me, I would avoid them and hope they would leave me alone so that I would not have to face the situation. I had terrible coping skills resulting from all the damage I had experienced.

My body was crying for help. My body displayed signs that all the suffering and negativity I had been experiencing was harmful. My anxiety was becoming a daily thing. I would break out in a sweat every time I got nervous about something. One day, I walked into work with my nice dress pants on and a casual designer shirt. I would wear a t-shirt under my shirt because I sweat so much. I got on the elevator and pressed button 10 to the company floor. I walked past a field of office cubicles to get to my desk. I had just about reached my desk, and my co-worker yelled, "Here comes the guy who loves the golden girls!" I was sweating all over the place because I was embarrassed. It was not a big deal, but the attention made me nervous.

I always carried a small towel with me everywhere I went because I would sweat at the drop of a hat. I felt awkward all the time for no reason. I didn't know what to do, so I did what I always have done. I avoided the issues, and I continued to live my life.

Becoming a therapist and using avoidance as a coping mechanism

I applied to Mercer University's clinical mental health master's program. The admission process was rigorous and very anxiety-provoking. I received a call from the university's receptionist that the admission staff wanted to interview me as a part of the acceptance process. I was exceptionally excited and anxious at the same time. The night before the interview, I was preparing myself mentally to address any questions that may have been presented to me. My anxiety was high. As I didn't want to miss this opportunity and wanted to be at my best, I did a mock interview with a friend of mine just to get the jitters out. "What made you want to become a therapist?" my friend asked in a silly voice. "I like to help people feel better about themselves." "Have you ever seen a therapist in your life?" my friend has now become serious with his questions. "No, I have not!" I was starting to get nervous as if I was in an actual interview. My hands were sweating. "Do you have any questions about the program?" he asked. "No, I have read about Mercer University and the clinical mental health program online." My friend and I did this mock interview for at least an hour. We prepared for every possible thing that could be asked in an interview. Also, in preparation for the interview, I laid out the outfit I was going to wear, and I placed my resume, my application, and unofficial transcripts from the previous college in my briefcase.

The following morning, I was up around 6 am with ruminating thoughts about how this interview would go. I thought to myself: Would I screw this up? What if I do not get accepted? Will they judge me based on my appearance, etc.....? My interview was scheduled for 9:30 am. The school was about 10 minutes away from my home, but I hated being late, so I left early. The drive to the school was very hectic that morning, there was the busy morning Atlanta traffic. I was looking at my watch as I drove down the highway. I was pondering thoughts about getting lost and not arriving on time; did I include everything I needed for the interview in my briefcase? I was sweating profusely because the air conditioning in my car was not working, and my nerves got the best of me. At each streetlight, I was nervously

41

tapping on the steering wheel, waiting for the streetlight to turn from red to green. This drive felt like an excruciating 8 hours of torture, but I arrived on time at 9 am.

The school was a coping mechanism for me to avoid life stressors. Going to school allowed me to hide by focusing on schoolwork and distracting myself from the negative life situations I had experienced. As a student, I would work my full-time job during the day and then take courses at night. If anyone asked me to go to a social event, my answer would be something like, "I have homework, I cannot go," but I felt like I was not living life. I only existed, but it was more comfortable and safer to stay at home away from people.

I am an anxious person. I made it to the campus and did not have any trouble locating the building. I walked into the counseling office and was greeted by the receptionist. Twenty-five minutes later, the receptionist escorted me to a large conference room where about ten professors from the counseling department sat glaring at me. I could feel my heart beating incredibly fast as if it was going to jump out of my chest. They all greeted me. "Do you have obsessive-compulsive disorder (OCD)?" one of the professors asked. Everyone laughed, but I felt awkward. "No, why do you ask?" I felt like I was going to pass out. My hands were sweating, and I could feel my heart pounding. "You are extra early for this interview," the professor gave me a stern look over his glasses. "I didn't want to be late," I responded nervously. The entire room broke out in laughter. After that, the interview went great!

I answered all the questions and addressed my experience with therapy and my mental health. I responded to the question about my mental health based on what I knew at the time of what mental health was. I was accepted into the program. Year one was fantastic! I learned about psychology and the stages of human development. Year two focused on learning behavioral theories and the theorist who created them. In year three, I learned how to conduct a therapy session. It was hard work, many writing papers, presentations, and being vulnerable with my colleagues. Three years later, I graduated from the program in 2013.

I learned so much about people and the world around me. I explored many theories from Freud to Alfred Adler, and I expected to utilize my education to heal my community. I wanted to be known as the wounded healer. I was hurt by all of my past negative life experiences, so I became a mental health therapist to help heal others from their mental illness; so that anyone else wouldn't face what I did. I believe that mental health treatment is a gift from God to help people talk about their struggles in a safe place. I wanted to be a facilitator in that safe space. I could use my trauma to educate my community about mental health illnesses. I continued to live my life. I had a great job, good friends, and a nice place to live. My family was okay at this point, so I assumed I was in a good place, but I avoided my mental health. Not only was school a coping avoidance mechanism, but so was exercise. It really helped me throughout the process.

Emotional eating was my coping mechanism:

Anxiety contributed to my emotions. My emotions were all over the place at times due to my overthinking about everything! I became a serial overthinker. My complexes overshadowed everything I succeeded in. My thoughts would tell me that to be successful, I had to be thin. To be successful, I had to be educated. To be rich, I had to work hard when everyone else was relaxing. To be in a relationship, I had to be thin! To be accepted, I had to be perfect! My thoughts controlled me, but eating was the resolution at the time. My burn trauma and its impact on my body were always present in my mind. I was an emotional eater due to anxiety.

It was a hot summer day, the grill was smoking, and the tables were covered with all types of food. Gospel music was playing in the background. The sound of laughter could be heard from blocks away. It was family day for my family. A day that we all came together to celebrate the family. My mom and my siblings would cook their favorite food dish and bring it to the event, which was held in our backyard.

My family would celebrate with food. Food helped us bond and not worry over the negative life situations. Growing up in my family, we celebrated all events with food, so in my mind, I correlated emotions with food. When things got stressful, food was my comfort. I remember when I had applied for a job I really wanted but did not get. I had prepared for the interview, I thought I did a good job in the interview, but then I received the email that I was not selected for the job. I ordered two cheese pizzas and ate both pizzas in one sitting. I was full, but I kept eating. When someone died, we celebrated their life with food.

On the other hand, food was also used to celebrate the good things in life. My family would get together during the summer and have a big neighborhood cookout. There would be all kinds of food. We had a great time! Food was my coping mechanism and gave me a sense of connection to family and community.

Extreme working out was my coping mechanism:

I avoided my anxiety-filled life as I got older by exercising. I started exercising in my first year of college because I was overweight. I had always struggled with my weight after I started middle school. I also experienced distorted body image issues. I enrolled in a physical fitness course, and this started my addiction to working out. I decided I needed to lose weight. I started drinking slim fast, working out to Richard Simmons's workout videos, and walking the local track. Exercising was my release and escape from reality. I would walk on the path for hours at a time, and eventually, I started losing weight. After the initial weight loss, it was hard to keep the weight off. I was on an up-and-down roller coaster with my weight, but exercising was my drug of choice.

I became an anxious Zumba instructor:

I loved working out so much that I became a Zumba instructor in 2011. I loved teaching Zumba; it was my therapy. I would attend every Zumba event because I was making new friends and the spirit of Zumba made me feel great. My class was the talk of the town. I felt like God had placed me in this position to help others feel good about themselves. I was glad that people truly loved my Zumba class.

My Zumba classes provided an escape from what was going on in the world. You could lose yourself in the music. It was fantastic! One student told me that my class was the only thing she had to look forward to in her life. Her husband had divorced her, and she was incredibly devasted. She started my classes after her divorce. I would hear stories like this after every class. This made me feel like a healer, and it made me feel good about the work I was doing. I wanted to help as many people as I could using Zumba. But in 2019, Zumba became a chore! I loved teaching my class, but the excitement for Zumba had decreased. I had too much going on.

I had a fear of being social. Living in Atlanta made me feel like I had to compete with all the perfect bodies I would see when I would attend events. My burn trauma and its impact on my body were always present in my mind. I remember going to an event, and everyone looked so nice. I was miserable, and I found the nearest corner to hide from myself from the crowd. I was 5'9", weighing 250. In my eyes, I was fat, but people would say I was thick, not fat. I felt fat; my clothes did not fit correctly; I had a lot of negative self-talk about myself during this event. I was clinging to my friends that I attended the event with, and I never reached out to talk to a stranger. I was terrified of being at parties.

My internal struggle:

Exercising was the way in which I escaped all of my ruminating anxious thoughts about my weight. It seemed that if I had gained a pound, someone in my circle of friends would comment that I was gaining weight. In my mind, when someone would say this, I would feel horrible. I felt like the worst person in the world. I could feel myself getting into deep with my body complexes. My anxiety had me believing that my life would be happier if I had a perfect weight. My intrusive thoughts went like this: "Fred, if you lose weight, people would like you better." "Fred, if you lose weight, you would be invited to more social events." "Fred, if you lose weight, you would be happier." "Fred, because you are overweight, nobody likes you." I would work out every day, sometimes twice a day. The feeling from working out was rejuvenating, but my weight was not going down. I knew the problem but found it hard to fix my emotional eating. I was binge eating.

Burn trauma and the perfect body:

My burn experience and its impact on my body were always present in my mind. It provoked my anxiety. The scars stared at me every day after I would take a shower. When I would look in the mirror, I would automatically see the big scar on my neck leading to the center of my chest. I was on a constant journey of making the "perfect body" despite the scars. In my mind, it did not matter if I lost weight or received compliments; there was always something that needed to be "fixed" related to my body.

On Saturdays, I would see my personal fitness trainer for an extra workout. Each night, I would consume a large meal because I hadn't eaten all day, and I would feel good because I had worked out hard and completed all my tasks. I was losing energy, but I was not losing weight because my body was incongruent with my mind. Meaning, I was working out to relieve the pressure of life, but I was emotionally eating. I was not burning more calories than I was taking in.

Speak Up Body

Life was crazy. I kept moving on

I didn't take the time to see what was wrong

Finally, my body got tired of being quiet

Anxiety spoke up to grab my attention

By Frederick Dare Brockington

Traveling to escape my life:

In the middle of everything that was going on during this time of my life, I went on a trip with my friends to Thailand and China. I was so excited. I was truly looking forward to the trip, but I was having ruminating thoughts about what could negatively happen to me on this trip. I was worried about catching a disease in a foreign country. I went to my doctor so that he could give me a hepatitis shot and malaria pills. I knew I would feel more comfortable traveling after I received these treatments. My friends were not freaking out about potential problems on the trip. They told me to calm down, and everything would be okay. I calmed down and booked the trip. I had never been out of the United States of America. This was going to allow me to see how people in other parts of the world lived. I visited Phuket Island,

49

Beijing, the Great Wall of China, and various other locations. Phuket Island was beautiful. It had blue water and these tall rocks that glimmered in the sun. In Beijing, the people seemed a little aggressive there, and they were moving rather quickly without an 'excuse me' or 'pardon me'. The Great Wall of China was beautiful. My friends and I took a tour up to the wall, and then we slid down the wall on the zig-zag slide. It was an amazing trip.

Chapter 4: Phobias

The anxious experience that changed my life:

I traveled home from Thailand to Atlanta, Georgia, but there was a layover at Los Angeles (LAX) airport. I had already been on a plane for at least 10 hours or more. My layover in LAX was for 6 hours. I had a lot of time to kill. I should have rented a hotel for the night, but I didn't want to stay the night in Los Angeles. I stayed at the airport for 6 hours. I slept on and off for most of the layover. I walked around the airport, grabbed some food, and played games on my phone. I thought to myself: The 4-hour flight from Los Angeles to Atlanta should be easy.

Hours later, it was time to board the flight. I preceded to get on the next flight, and everything was fine. My seat was the window seat, which I loved. I stared out the window to see all the fluffy white clouds. My row was full, so there was someone in the middle seat and the aisle seat. The seating arrangement was not a problem at the time. After 3 hours had passed, the passenger sitting beside me had fallen asleep on my shoulder. I was asleep myself but woke up in a panic with my heart beating fast. I was sweating profusely! The feeling was unbearable! I had never felt this feeling before. I felt like I needed to open the airplane door and just start free falling to get away from this feeling. I felt confined and wanted to break free. The passengers beside me looked at me as if I was crazy. I jumped up out of my seat, went to the back of the airplane, and asked the flight attendant if I could stay back there until I calmed down.

The flight attendants seemed a little worried about me, but once I explained that I had a racing heartbeat and sweating, they allowed me to stay with them in the back of the plane. "It's probably a panic attack," one of the flight attendants stated. "This type of thing happens to a lot of people." In my mind, I was thinking: "This has never happened to me." They gave me water, and I stood in the back with them for about thirty minutes, trying to calm myself down. The plane was about to land, and they told me I had to go back to my seat for the landing. I asked the passengers who I was sitting by if they could slide down. I didn't want to sit in the window seat because I didn't feel well. They nicely slid down so that I could have a seat in the aisle. I finally relaxed, and the flight was over.

I didn't understand this experience at all. I asked myself what had happened to me. I didn't understand what these feelings were, and I didn't understand where these feelings came from. My body was trying to tell me something. When I did research, my symptoms fit the definition of claustrophobia.

What are you afraid of? I got off the plane in disbelief. I was usually not afraid of flying. What just happened? Are you losing it? I had discussed panic attacks and anxiety during my master's program, but when you are experiencing it yourself, it is hard to identify. If I were to tell my family or friends about this situation I just had, they would have called me crazy, I thought. I didn't mention this issue to anyone at the time. I acted as if it did not happen, but as soon as I got home, I decided to look up mental health issues and found the words claustrophobia and anxiety. A lot of people on the internet described having a similar feeling. I didn't feel so bad, but I felt ashamed that this had happened to me. I wanted to have the perfect persona.

My phobia:

A phobia is a type of anxiety that is an irrational, unreasonable fear of an object or situation. I had just experienced claustrophobia and a panic attack at the same time. I had a fear of restriction on an airplane. Specific phobias are persistent and excessive or unreasonable fear when in the presence of or when anticipating an encounter with a particular object or situation. A specific phobia is a fear reaction when confronted with an object or situation. Symptoms of claustrophobia include,

- sweating and chills
- accelerated heart rate and high blood pressure
- dizziness, fainting, and lightheadedness
- dry mouth

- hyperventilation or "over-breathing."
- hot flashes
- shaking or trembling and a sense of "butterflies" in the stomach
- nausea
- headache
- numbness
- a choking sensation
- tightness in the chest, chest pain, and difficulty breathing
- an urge to use the bathroom
- confusion or disorientation
- fear of harm or illness

The act of worrying involves negative images, irrational fears, appearing in your memory that something will hurt you or someone around you, and worry is a component of anxiety. Why was I having this fear in my life suddenly? When did it happen, and why did it happen? Here I was, in my forties, facing overwhelming feelings about certain situations that were placed in my life – where did this begin?

My coping mechanism for my phobia:

Was the fear I had felt in confined spaces going to keep happening to me, or was this a one-time thing? I had so many unanswered questions, but again, I avoided the issues and went on with my life. However, I had to make sure I was not putting myself in a position to be confined for fear of this happening again. That included avoiding situations such as long car rides, sitting between two people in a movie theater, taking the elevator, and making sure I selected the seat at the end of the row so I could easily get up if I needed to escape or move around. Unfortunately, this coping mechanism did not work.

My panic attacks:

One afternoon, I was preparing for a speech for one of my college courses when all of a sudden, I had heart palpitations, my heart started beating really fast, pounding out of control, and I began to sweat profusely. I could not control what was happening to me. I was scared that I may have suffered a heart attack. All I could imagine was me collapsing on the floor due to a heart attack. I was not sure what was going on with my body, but I knew it felt strange. I felt out of control. I sat down for a minute and gathered my composure. I quieted the negative self-talk I was experiencing during that moment. Negative self-talk is when your thoughts are negative towards yourself. "Fred, you are dying? Fred, you are being squished to death. Fred, you are losing it." I realized that my symptoms were only feelings, and the only thing I could tell that was physically happening was the fast heartbeat and sweating. After a while, I ignored the feelings, and they went away. My heartbeat slowed down once I calmed down.

Visited a physician:

A month later, the same feelings and the fast heartbeat returned. I was freaking out! What was going on? I visited all kinds of doctors to get an answer. I visited my primary doctor and then a cardiologist. I did the stress test on the treadmill. I had a complete physical. I had a family history of diabetes and strokes, so I thought they surely would have found something to explain what was happening to me.

"Mr. Brockington, the doctor says there is nothing abnormal about your test results." I was confused to hear this at every visit. Every test result came back negative, but the heart palpitations, fear, and panic remained. The feelings and the symptoms of my attack would appear periodically. I thought to myself: Am I losing my mind? What is happening to me? I felt alone and scared and did not feel like myself. I felt like my life was over as I knew it. I was so caught up in what was happening to me that I didn't think about my mental health training. The statement everyone says is that the therapist is the worst patient.

What is happening to me? Had my life come to a standstill? Had I had all the fun I would ever have because this thing was happening to me? I could not do anything about it. I refused to let my friends and family know what was happening to me because I could not explain it myself.

I was ashamed of experiencing something I could not explain.

Ashamed of My Feelings

The strange feeling won't go away

I am so ashamed of it I can't even say

To my family and my friends, this is happening to me

I kept quiet about the feelings inside of me

Dr. Frederick Dare Brockington

Chapter 5: Exploration Of Mental Health In The Black Community

Black and Brown mental health:

Amid my own struggles, I am now a therapist! After everything I have been through, I am finally living a better life with good mental health. The World Health Organization (WHO) defines good mental health as every one's ability to cope with everyday stressors of life and still contribute to the success of their communities. One of the goals I had set for myself was to give back to the Black community as it relates to educating them on how important therapy is. I wanted to let them know that the level of necessity we have for doctors, we have it for the therapist as well. I wanted to make sure Black men and women sought therapy earlier in their lives after a sad or adverse life event rather than later. First, I had to understand the problems in the Black community that could lead to higher levels of stress and anxiety.

Black individuals and mental health:

Black individuals are more likely to experience mental health illness due to high unemployment levels, discrimination, poverty, and disruptions in family functioning. As a therapist, I have seen Black males who have experienced negative life events and tried to move on with their lives without any professional help, and I can tell you that attempting to move on does not work. These Black males usually turn to substance abuse to cope with the additional stressors of life.

Black sadness, hopelessness, and worthlessness:

The data shows that Black people are more likely to experience sadness, hopelessness, and worthlessness than Whites, and Black teenagers are more likely to commit suicide. Within some Black communities, individuals are striving for survival, dealing with Black-on-Black crimes, racism, and other daily life and economic stressors, which can create minority stress.

Minority Stress

Jr. interviewed for a new job and was hired. He was anxious and excited about the job, but he knew very little about the work environment. He started on Monday at 8 am. He drove to the office, parked, and walked through the main door. He was met by his supervisor and escorted to his desk. Jr. noticed that he was the only Black person on the team. None of his new co-workers would speak to him or look him in the eyes. If he asked a question, they would refer him to his supervisor. Jr. was stressed by this new work environment and eventually quit the job. Minority stress is distinctive stress experienced by racial minorities due to racial prejudice and the economic disadvantages faced by Black individuals.

Unique stressors faced by Blacks:

Black males in America have unique stressors that impact their mental health over their life span. Black males also experience higher high school dropout rates, incarceration, homelessness, unemployment, depression, substance abuse, and homicide, but Black males seek professional mental health treatment at lower rates than any other racial group.

Racialized Trauma

Racialized trauma is race-based stress generated from encounters with racial bias and ethnic discrimination, racism, and hate crimes. Historical dehumanization, present-day racism, mass trauma, human loss, and grief are some of the issues the Black community continues to experience. Neighborhoods filled with killings, robberies, police brutality can be traumatizing.

Police brutality

Police brutality against Black people is the current-day slave control technique. Police believe that if they put fear into people of color, they can control them. Currently, the spotlight has been on police brutality. A lot of unarmed Black people have died at the hands of police officers. This is the current-day dehumanization of Black people.

George Floyd:

As I was writing this book in 2020, I heard the news that a police officer in Minnesota murdered George Floyd. He was accused of using counterfeit currency. A police officer held George Floyd down by placing his knee on Floyd's neck. The George Floyd killing traumatized the world, specifically Black and Brown people. Sadly, police brutality against Brown and Black people in the United States continues to be a problem.

Ahmaud Arbery:

Not only are cops targeting Black men, but so are Caucasian citizens who feel they are entitled and privileged. These citizens decided that Ahmaud was a threat simply because he decided to look at a new house being constructed. An ex-cop and his son killed Ahmaud Arbery for "looking" like a suspect. A sentiment in most of the United States of America is that Black males are a target for police officers. I find myself feeling anxious and sad about living in the United States. Racialized trauma is a real thing. It is easy for people to look down on others when they have never had to experience such a negative life leading back to slavery.

Trauma and Slavery

Slavery has created past trauma experiences for all Black people. I believe the trauma has been passed down from generation to generation. Slavery is a generational curse.

Slavery trauma cannot be seen with the naked eye. I believe it is unconscious negativity suppression in every Black person, and it is triggered by racism. I believe the entire world is impacted by slavery and racism. Trauma never goes away! It must be processed from the unconscious to the conscious.

Subconscious slave trauma:

Our ancestors placed their traumatic experiences in their subconscious as they related to slavery. A friend of mine informed me of a book called *Post Traumatic Slave Syndrome* by Dr. Joy DeGruy. This book discusses the residual effects of generations of enslavement to Black people in America. I truly believe that a lot of African Americans' mental health issues come from the fact that our ancestors experienced slavery and were never given a chance to process this trauma. For example, our ancestors were forced to take care of others, and some of them were whipped, raped, and traumatized. They were never able to process this trauma; they had to grin and bear it. The only therapy they had was praying and singing old Negro spirituals. Does this sound familiar? This is what our community continues to do. We go through so much but never take the time to acknowledge that we are hurt, bruised, and battered. We do not admit we are in pain, and we pass this avoidance tactic on to our children.

Iyania, fix my life:

I was watching an episode of *Iyania, Fix My Life,* on the OWN Network. There was an older lady from the South who was very mean and hateful to her daughter. They would get into physical fights, and the mom would call her daughter horrible names. The daughter hated her mom and moved out of the house as soon as possible. Well, the daughter repeated the same behaviors to her daughter but much worse. The generational curse passed down. The resolution to this situation was to explore the mother's past. The mother grew up during a racist time and everything that was done to her by the racist people she did to her daughter. The daughter had no idea this was the case and felt bad about hating her mother. She then apologized to her daughters for her behavior. I mention this true story to show that the past must be explored to move forward.

Learned behaviors:

The *Iyania, Fix My Life* story is a perfect example of how the behaviors we learn during our traumatic experiences could reappear later in life without our consent; this is called traumatic reenactment. I see many clients who experience traumatic reenactment, and until they become aware that this is happening, they will never change the behavior.

Black People Need Therapy

If black people experience great amounts of sadness, hopelessness, worthlessness, minority stress, slave trauma, and police brutality, why don't they seek mental health therapy? I provided my reasons in the previous chapter, and I created what I believe are the main reasons therapy may not be an option.

Black people have a higher risk of anxiety. Due to the exposure to poverty, substance misuse, delinquency, violence exposure, and discrimination, Black children and adolescents are placed at higher risk of anxiety and depression. The way we cope with or manage our trauma determines whether we experience anxiety or not. Therefore, some people may be impacted by their negative life events, and some may not.

How trauma turns into anxiety:

Psychologists have found that traumatic life events are the major cause of anxiety and depression. The severity of this anxiety and depression is based on how the individuals think about the events. Other causes of anxiety are family history of mental health issues, income and education levels, relationship issues, and social factors.

Reasons Why Black People Do Not Seek Therapy

There are three main reasons why some Black people do not seek mental health treatment: There is a stigma in the Black community related to mental health treatment, and some Black people believe they cannot afford mental health treatment. Thirdly, there is a lack of knowledge regarding mental health illness in the Black community.

1. The Stigma:

Some Black people do not believe in mental health issues or seek mental health treatment. Some Black people do not seek mental health treatment due to stigma and misinformation about mental health. The stigma creates a barrier to having a conversation around mental health illness. Whenever someone lets others know that they are seeking professional help, we, in an instant, make a perception about them being eccentric. Some Black families believe mental health illness is a demonic spirit that must be cast out. Some Black families believe prayer and meditation will help eradicate your mental health illness, and you do not need to see a therapist. As a Black male in the Black community, I have always heard. Black people fear therapy because the Black community will look down on them as being crazy, disturbed, or off.

The weird lady:

I remember when I was around 10 years old, I observed a Black female walking around a tree in my neighborhood. She was talking to herself. She acted as if she was not in her "right mind." I saw her several times throughout the neighborhood doing strange things. Her actions were a little peculiar to me, so I asked my big sister, "What is wrong with that lady?" My sister said, "She was at a party, and someone slipped something in her drink, and she has never been the same!" This was the rumor around the neighborhood regarding this individual. I never asked any more questions, and this was going to be my response if anyone ever asked me that question about the same lady. I look back on that situation and wonder if this lady had a mental health issue that was disguised by the neighborhood story.

The strange church lady:

Another incident in my neighborhood was when I was attending church, and there was a church family member everyone would consider "strange." She would sit in church and stare into space. We would not see a lot of her, but when we did, it seemed like something was "off." It seems like my community and my church avoided the discussion of discussing mental health issues. My community would use words to describe people who were different with words like strange, crazy, and mentally off. No one would ever discuss the topic of mental health, which is why I believe this creates the stigma of mental health.

You are not crazy:

Having a mental health illness does not mean you are crazy! Mental health illness must be treated by a mental health professional but searching for a therapist you feel comfortable seeing can be problematic. I struggled with finding a therapist who would not judge me and a therapist who was not a male. But every Black individual is different and has different needs.

Culturally competent stigma:

When I was searching for a therapist, I wanted a Caucasian therapist due to my past negative life history. This is not the case for all Black individuals. For Black individuals who have had a lot of racial trauma, there is mistrust of a non-Black therapist. The Black individual may feel like the non-Black therapist is not culturally competent to provide mental health treatment.

Black language versus the provider's language:

Some Black people feel the non-Black therapist misinterprets their language during the session. Some Black people fear that the non-Black therapist will create trouble for them or their family if they provide certain information during a session. Some Black families simply do not trust an outsider with their personal family information, so they would rather have the family member suffer in silence. Once Black individuals get over this hurdle, the financial aspect of mental health treatment is a problem.

2. Can't Afford Mental Health Treatment:

The second reason some Black individuals do not attend therapy is the lack of finances. Some Black families in poverty-stricken rural areas cannot afford mental health treatment due to lack of money, no insurance, no time due to working full-time, or the lack of transportation to travel to the mental health office. Rural areas are not equipped to support the mental health needs of Black children because of economic oppression and racism.

Some Black families struggle with putting food on the table, clothing themselves, and providing other basic life needs. Mental health therapy would therefore be a luxury. When some Black boys are diagnosed with mental health disorders within rural areas by a school therapist, their families cannot afford proper mental health treatment. Of the 10-12% of Black children and adolescents with mental disorders, only one-quarter of them receive appropriate mental health services. Black individuals living below the poverty level are twice likely to report mental health issues as those living over the poverty level. I am not saying the mental health disparity does not exist in urban areas but based on my experiences; I see it a lot more in the rural areas.

Some Black families in the urban areas seem to be able to provide mental health treatment for their children if the services are needed.

Free "therapy":

Going to church was my therapy growing up. I loved going to church. It was a family affair. I loved the church environment because it was stress-free. It felt like my second home. The church environment had everything I needed: my family, my friends, singing in the choir, after-service dinners, baked church goods, and the neighborhood store we would run to after service was over to get candy.

I would get dressed up in my Sunday suit and my shiny black shoes every Sunday. My family and I would make that drive to the church, which was about 10 minutes away. I would carry my Sunday school book with me because I would get into trouble if I forgot it. I attended Sunday school, where I learned a lot of parables about God's life. I was always excited about meeting up with my church friends and reciting bible scriptures. There were a lot of Christmas plays and vacation Bible school. I do not know why but I loved these things growing up. I learned about the power of God, and I established a relationship with God at an early age.

My mother, father, and the church taught my siblings and me to pray to God to heal us from whatever was bothering us. We depended on our faith in God to heal our physical and mental health issues. At the time, I believed the philosophy that God heals all things. When someone got sick, we prayed day and night until they were healed. Even though we had faith in God, somehow, we ended up at the doctor's office if someone's health took a turn for the worst. Looking back at this, I realized there was some hypocrisy in believing that God healed all things. Today, I still believe in God and have a relationship with him, but I believe he has given us doctors, nurses, and therapists to help cure and heal our diseases.

Religious faith and common sense: My religious background is Pentecostal. The Pentecostal religion believes we must have faith in God and the Holy Spirit. We believe God, the Father, the Son, and the Holy Spirit are one. As a Pentecostal believer, your faith in God is the controlling factor of your life. I continue to have my strong faith in God and that God protects and guides me in my day-to-day life. I also believe that God gave us common sense to use the tools that are available to us. This scenario has created the stigma and a lack of knowledge of mental health issues in the Black community. It is very dangerous to tell people in a blanket statement to rely on God to treat their mental health issues without knowing what type of mental health illness they are experiencing. For example, if someone is suffering from suicidal thoughts without treatment, they are in danger of killing themselves. There are different levels of depression, some more severe than others.

3. Lack of Knowledge:

A lot of Black boys and girls may be experiencing severe depression but are told that they are sad or are just having a bad day. I keep repeating this, so people can understand that more education is needed on mental health issues in the Black community. In Jr.'s story, he did not identify he was experiencing mental health issues. Jr. assumed that when someone dies, you are sad all the time. To be honest, until I became a mental health therapist, I didn't realize what mental health illness entailed. I believed mental health illness consisted of people who talked to themselves and saw things that were not there. I believed people were either sad or happy because of something that happened in their lives. I believed that over time, the person who experienced something negative in their lives would just "get over it." I didn't realize that past trauma could reappear in my life as well as the lives of others. I decided to become a mental health therapist to provide mental health services to all and educate my own people. I decided to define the concepts of trauma, anxiety, and phobia to inform the readers of this book on these concepts from a mental health perspective.

Therapy is for White people:

The only time I would hear the word therapy or hear about people going to therapy was the rich White people I saw on television. Seeing therapy on television made me think that going to therapy was not a reality. In my eyes, things on television did not equate to what I did in my life. I do not recall a lot of television shows that featured Black people attending therapy. In 2020, few shows were identified as shows featuring Black families who addressed mental health conversation, and they are Giants, This is us, and She's Gotta have it. I am glad that things are changing.

Church and therapy:

Often, in the Black community, we are told to pray about the health problem, the divorce, the troubled child, the cheating boyfriend or girlfriend, or the inability to pay bills. This list could go on and on. Pray for healing. Does this sound familiar? There is nothing wrong with prayer, but we must use God's common sense when we are not feeling well. I thought that these feelings I was experiencing had something to do with my mental health, but I didn't know the definition of mental health illness. Specifically, I didn't know what mental health illness looked like in a Black boy like myself. The only thing I knew about mental health was people talking to themselves and displaying erratic behavior. We had never discussed mental health in my family or my community. The lack of discussion regarding mental health was not anyone's fault; it was the fact we had other things to worry about in our community.

The Pew survey stated that 18% of African Americans describe their religious identity as agnostic, atheist, or with no affiliation with the church. Recently, NFL football player Arian Foster stated that he does not believe in God and has faith that does not work for him. Religion has been defined as a cultural system of beliefs, practices, and rituals that govern the universe. At the same time, spirituality is associated with a person's connectivity to the transcendent and supernatural.

Protect your mental and physical health! Cultural expectations for Black males are that they show emotional toughness, pride, autonomous coping, and maintaining self-control, despite any mental or physical issues. I subconsciously thought that if I expressed my feelings, I would be considered weak by my male counterparts. I lived my life by this cultural expectation of showing no emotions. I remember in middle school, my best friend and I got into a fight because he kept teasing me, which is something we did to each other all the time. But when everyone else started picking on me and saying I was weak for letting him tease me, I had to show I was tough, so I fought him to prove that I was stronger.

Deep inside, I didn't want to fight my best friend, but I was peer pressured into doing it. We both were punished and placed in after-school suspension. I was protecting myself in the school environment because I could not protect myself in my home environment. I had a lot of emotions going on at the time. I was anxious that people would notice my burns, and I tried to keep up the image of not being weak and showing emotions. Black boys and girls, please be open and vulnerable with your family. It is okay to express what you are going through. It hurts my heart to see grown men come into therapy not knowing how to express their problems or mental health because they were taught that it was not okay. The inability for Black boys to express their emotions is because our ancestors were slaves and did not have a voice. The males did the hard labor and could not express emotions on how they felt about it, or they would have to pay the price. This negative experience left its effect on the Black community in the United States.

Hello Black boys and girls, you have made it this far. I hope you have learned what anxiety is. I hope you have learned that your trauma is not going to go away. I hope you realize you must process, learn coping skills, welcome support, and make meaning out of every negative experience before moving to the next phase of your life. I hope you have learned that anxiety is more than just a nervous feeling. I hope you have learned that there are different types of anxiety. I hope you educate your family about mental health and engage with them in a family discussion about treatment and treatment options.

Seeking

Seeking to find help is hard to do

You have to trust your life with a total stranger

With the secret details about yourself

But in the end, you will win

by seeking help to allow your soul to mend

By Dr. Frederick Brockington

Chapter 6: Trying To Find A Mental Health Solution

Mixed emotions out of control:

Black men, have you ever experienced the need to be perfect? A conflict with who you are compared to what you are? A feeling of panic, fear, anxiousness, loss of control, not feeling like yourself, and you could not explain it? You may have thought that you had everything under control in your life, and then suddenly, things changed. You felt like somewhere in this life journey, the courageous individual you once were is now very anxious. These feelings were my "normal." I thought I had anxiety, but I was not sure. I was unsure what anxiety was, but I often used the word when I described the negative feelings I had. I was on a search for what was going on with me.

I was searching for answers. I didn't know what I was experiencing, but I thought it was anxiety. I wanted someone to give me an answer. I didn't want to go to the doctor, but I was curious how my Facebook friends would define anxiety. I posted on my Facebook page, *what does anxiety mean to you?* I had assumed that people believed anxiety meant to worry or to be scared about something.

At first, I didn't think anyone would respond because most people do not like talking about their mental health, especially on social media. To my surprise, I received a reasonable number of responses. There were twenty responses received from my Facebook friends. The racial makeup of the participants was: 7 Black females, 8 Black males, 1 White male, and 4 White females. An analysis of the responses identified several themes.

Nervousness:

One common theme was the word **nervousness**. People equated anxiety with feeling nervous or panicky about something and not knowing what to expect. I was nervous all the time. I always expected something negative to happen, so I made sure I was fully prepared in any situation I was about to take on. I remember one night that I was supposed to go on a date, but I had canceled it because I was nervous about whether or not they would like me due to my weight. I didn't go on a date.

Fear:

Another theme that frequently appeared in the responses was the word **fear**. Fear of the unknown was all I knew at this stage in my life. If I didn't know all the details about a situation, I would be in so much fear that I would not participate in the event or the situation. I would constantly back out of an engagement because the fear of failure would take over without even having any evidence.

Control your anxiety:

Several individuals stated that anxiety needed to be managed. These individuals felt like anxiety could get out of control if that person did not seek mental health treatment. My "anxiety" at this point in my life felt out of control. I became introverted. I didn't hang out with my friends as much because I felt like I was only in control of my life within the four walls of my apartment. I could control the situation in my apartment, control the apartment's temperature, control who I talked to, and control the food I ate, and I felt safe from any strange things.

Handle anxiety with drugs:

Another common theme amongst the Black male respondents to my Facebook post was that they used marijuana to cope with their anxious feelings. Escapism is a real thing. A lot of people turn to drugs to deal with their reality. The problem is that Black men are more likely to be punished criminally because of this. Existing literature shows that Black males use marijuana to deal with psychological distress and racial discrimination. My drugs of choice to calm my negative emotions were food and exercise. If I were having a bad day, I would emotionally eat. If I were feeling overly anxious, I would go to the gym to relieve the feelings. Also, Black males considered anxiety as a feeling they experience in their everyday lives.

Men and women's anxious emotions:

After reviewing the Facebook responses, it was interesting to see the differences between the male's and the female's definitions of anxiety. The male answers seemed to lack emotion related to anxiety, while the female responses were full of emotion. For example, a few male responses indicated that anxiety is a part of life; stop being a cry baby and pray to God. The women's responses identified how life-changing anxiety could be emotional. My thoughts were all over the place. The thing I called "anxiety" continued to be a strange concept. Continuing my search for what anxiety was, I decided to research the definition of anxiety.

Less likely to seek treatment for anxiety:

After years of feeling like I wasn't in control of my life, the out-of-control feeling became normal for me. I accepted the fact that I was going to break out into a panic if something new was presented to me. I didn't want anyone to know my secret problem, so I didn't seek treatment. African Americans are less likely to seek treatment for anxiety symptoms because they have normalized the symptoms. Is this the reason why Black males do not seek treatment? Because they believe anxiety and other mental health issues are just a part of life? I continued to experience emotions and feelings that made me uncomfortable. If I was irritated with myself, I didn't want to be around others.

Chapter 7: Anxiety

Experts Define Anxiety

According to researchers, anxiety is a built-in response system that impacts behavior, as well as cognitive and physiological responses, with worrying being the consequence of anxiety. Anxiety is the anxious nervousness or fear towards a situation, event, relationship, or an individual for an unknown reason. Anxiety sensitivity is the fear which can be uncontrollable and have harmful psychological or social consequences. I wanted to know how this "anxiety" thing impacted my body physically and identify the different types of anxiety.

Different Types of Anxiety

Anxiety comes in all shapes and sizes. As reported by Harvard Health Publishing: Harvard Medical School, the list of anxiety disorders is:

- **Generalized anxiety disorder** - Dramatic worry about health, money, safety, and daily life stressors lasting six months or more. Muscle pain, headaches, fatigue, nausea, issues with breathing, and trouble sleeping usually follow the previous symptoms. I have a lot of clients who experience generalized anxiety. They fear the unknown in many situations. For example, my clients have a lot of fear due to the pandemic because the result of their existence is unknown if they happen to get sick. Or, they feel incredibly anxious about a change to their lives they were not expecting.

- **Social anxiety disorder** - Overwhelming self-consciousness in ordinary social encounters, heightened by a sense of being watched and judged by others and a fear of embarrassment. According to the Psychology & Psychiatry Journal, social anxiety disorder (SAD) is the persistent excessive terror and avoidance of social and performance situations. I only developed social anxiety when I got older. For example, singing in front of people used to be fun when I was younger, but as I got older, I sweated profusely, and my body tremors. It is no longer fun to sing in front of people because my social anxiety makes me feel horrible.

- **Post-traumatic stress disorder (PTSD)** - Reliving an intense physical or emotional threat or injury (for example, childhood abuse, combat, or an earthquake) in vivid dreams, flashbacks, or tormented memories. Other symptoms include difficulty sleeping or concentrating, angry outbursts, emotional withdrawal, and a heightened startle response. An example of PTSD is when a person sees another person die in a car accident. The person who saw the accident becomes fearful of riding in a car because it triggers the negative experience they remember.

- **Obsessive/Compulsive Disorder (OCD)** - Obsessive thoughts, such as an irrational fear of contamination, are accompanied by compulsive acts, such as repetitive hand washing, that are undertaken to alleviate the anxiety generated by the thoughts. An example of OCD is when a person has obsessive thoughts of making all the light switches in the house be in the same direction. They will check the switches repeatedly to ensure that the light switches are in the same direction.

- **Panic disorder** - Recurrent episodes of unprovoked feelings of terror or impending doom, accompanied by rapid heartbeat, sweating, dizziness, or weakness. Anxiety can create physical illnesses such as substance abuse, physical addiction, irritable bowel syndrome (IBS), migraine headaches, heart disease, chronic respiratory disorders, and gastrointestinal conditions. I have had a panic attack getting a Cardiac MRI X-ray. When my doctor placed me in the Cardiac MRI machine, I could not stop shaking and sweating profusely, and I could not complete the X-ray. My heart was beating so fast that the machine could not get a good reading.

- **Phobias** - Irrational fear of specific things or situations, such as spiders (arachnophobia), being in crowds (agoraphobia), or being in enclosed spaces (claustrophobia). I have experienced claustrophobia. I cannot stand being in enclosed spaces. For example, I cannot sit in the backseat of a small car, or I will have a panic attack. I cannot sit in the center of a booth at a restaurant without freaking out. My dentist's office building is on the 7th floor. One day, I approached the elevator, and suddenly a fear came over me. I started getting anxious, and thoughts of getting stuck on the elevator ran across my mind. I began to panic. I told myself I had to get my teeth cleaned, so I must get on the elevator now. I challenged myself and made it to the 7th floor successfully. It was a relief, but after the appointment, I had to rechallenge myself to take the elevator down, and it was successful. I currently manage all of these symptoms by challenging my thoughts.

You may be worrying a lot, but something is triggering it. What type of anxiety do you have? It could be the fear of confined spaces, which is claustrophobia, or that you are nervous about standing in front of a crowd, which is social anxiety. In both scenarios, anxiety is the common denominator. Utilize the list to identify which type of anxiety may be impacting you. Now we know that there are different types of anxiety, let's explore how it connects to our trauma.

Symptoms of Anxiety

There are many symptoms of anxiety. Some of the symptoms include sensitivity, as well as physical, social, separation, and harm avoidance. According to the United

Kingdom National Health Service (NHS), some of the physical symptoms of general anxiety disorder are:

- stomach discomfort
- nausea, or digestive issues
- dizziness
- fatigue
- heart palpitations
- muscle pain and tightness
- trembling
- dry mouth
- extreme sweating
- shortness of breath
- feeling sick
- headache
- pins and needles

The Physical Impacts of Anxiety

For Black people, anxiety is not just being nervous. The anxious feelings start in a part of the brain called the amygdala (emotional brain), which is responsible for emotional responses. The neurotransmitters then carry the anxiety impulses to the nervous system. Other researchers believe anxiety is caused by the constant communication (a fear network) of different brain regions. A person feels anxiety when the emotional brain overpowers the cognitive brain in the frontal lobe, where all our sensations and thoughts come together. Anxiety is not all bad -- it prepares the body for a crisis if one is about to arise. What these definitions indicate to me is that anxiety is not just a feeling. Anxiety causes your body to function differently, so for those who think anxiety is all mental, that is not true.

Anxiety impacted my social relationships

Anxiety had taken over at this point. I was incredibly anxious, and I do not think I was a good friend to most people during this time. My friendships were not doing well. I had known Tony for more than 20 years. I had known Macy for 13 years. I had known John for 10 years, and I had known Eli for 25 years. Tony and I met in college and helped each other with homework assignments, breakups, choir, and financial problems. If I needed something to eat and did not have any money, Tony would lend it to me and vice versa. We would hang out at each other's houses during college breaks and holidays.

Something changed!

Years later, once college was over, Tony moved back home to New York, and I stayed in Atlanta. "Fred, I am coming to visit!" Tony said with excitement in his voice. "I don't think that is a good idea. I am extremely busy with school and work." I was very irritated and did not want to be bothered by anyone. "Oh, you're acting differently now that you have new friends in Atlanta." Tony was overly annoyed with me. "No, it's not like that, I am really busy," I said in a panicky voice. Tony's calls became fewer and fewer after this incident. I was awkward to be around. I didn't trust myself or the friends around me for safety. I felt like all the people I was close to for years became problematic. I felt like I was growing apart from long-time friends and vice versa. I felt like my friends did not like me anymore.

Questioning myself

I often asked myself, *"Was I horrible to be around, or was I doing something to people, and I didn't realize it?"* Macy lived right around the corner from me. She would just drop by my house anytime she wanted when we first met, and it was great at the time. But I didn't like her just dropping by as I got older. Knock, knock, knock! "Who is it?" I asked with annoyance. "Macy!" she replied. "What do you want? I am not ready for visitors." I wanted her to go away. "I am sorry, I thought it was okay to drop by to see how you were doing," Macy said with sadness and anger in her voice. "It was okay in the beginning, but I would like you to text me first because I get anxious about the way my house looks when visitors stop by unannounced." I tried to cover up my annoyance that Macy was at my door. "Okay!" I could hear Macy slam her car door. She stopped coming by and calling altogether.

The loss-of-a-close-friend scenario had happened multiple times. Anxiety prevented me from being vulnerable. I was always the take-charge person—the person who had it together. I now realize that taking charge was my coping mechanism for anxiety that I had developed a long time ago. I didn't let my friends into my world of anxiety. I always find myself hiding things about myself from the people I love. I developed the coping skill of handling things on my own and avoidance.

Broken friendships

I ran into an old friend, John, in a club. "Hey Fred, this is John!" I gave him a puzzled look. "Hey John, how are you?" I said in an unsure voice. "I have been calling you, but you have not answered your phone. Why?" John was irritated with me! "I have been experiencing a lot of personal issues like deaths in the family and trying to figure out my life." I was irritated with John! I wanted him to leave me alone. "I understand, but you could at least answer the phone and let me know you are okay." I was embarrassed by my behavior, and I held my head down. "Sorry, I didn't think about that." I was ready for this conversation to be over. We began to grow distant from each other, and I felt like we were not close anymore. My anxiety had gotten the best of me, and I became more introverted. No matter what we tried to do to mend our relationship, I felt like we could never achieve the type of friendship we had in the past. I visited him in Texas, but he seemed like he was disengaged with my presence. We hung out, but it was a fake friendship at this point. I realized John did not like me anymore, and I needed to pull back. My anxiety had me worrying for years that I had done something wrong.

Keeping negative relationships

I had become a people pleaser and did what I needed to maintain friendships. I was always giving. I was always the one who paid for things. I was always the one who got the short end of the stick. I was fearful that people would not like me if I didn't pay for things. At one point, I was preparing for an upcoming cruise I had purchased for my graduation. The cruise started on Thursday and lasted until the following Thursday. My best friend Eli and I were up early, excited about the trip. In the past, I had paid for cruises for others so that I would not have to cruise alone. We boarded the ship with drinks in our hands. I wanted to walk the ship and see what was happening, but my friend was on the phone talking to his other friends, and when he was not doing that, he was talking to all the other cruise passengers. We no longer had anything in common. I didn't have a good time, because I was with someone I only *thought* was my friend. Due to my anxiety, I couldn't see that the people I called friends were not good for me. Anxiety had taken control of my life.

Another panic attack in front of my friends

My friends and I were heading to Florida on a road trip. I was sitting in the back seat when suddenly, I felt the need to get out of the car. I asked my friend, who was driving, stopping the car because I felt strange. My friends were afraid and asked me if I was okay. My heart was beating fast, and I was shaking and sweating profusely. I had another anxiety attack. My friends did not know about any of the previous ones. I walked around for a while and then asked the person sitting in the front to see if we could exchange seats. I sat in the front seat, and we arrived safely with no other issues.

My body was tired of being ignored

Looking back on my trip home from Thailand, there was a lesson to be learned. The message was to pay attention to my mental health! Something happened to me mentally on this trip. At this point, my anxiety was SCREAMING at me. The trip was exceptionally long, over 18 hours, to be exact. I was exhausted; I needed some rest, and I was stressed from the long journey. I didn't give my body what it wanted, which was rest. Rest from being physically and mentally drained. I knew I was safe, and there was nothing to fear, but my body told me something was wrong.

Stop and pay attention

For many years, I had experienced the symptoms of sweating profusely when I was nervous. I used to sweat when I was younger, but now it was a lot more, and I was starting to shake badly along with it. The panic attack changed my life. I noticed that each year after my Thailand trip, my nervous feelings increased. I felt embarrassed and ashamed of the feelings that fear brought on by an invisible thing. But my level of nervousness was different. It was beginning to impact my functioning in my work and social environments. I said to myself, *"Houston, we have a problem."* I had panic attacks often at this point.

Panic attack

My anxiety was getting out of control. After the initial claustrophobia attack, I experienced more attacks. I had an attack in the back of an Uber ride with my Zumba students there to experience it. I had only coffee that morning before teaching my Zumba class. My students, Shaneese, Ebony, and Carlo, wanted to attend an event after class, so I agreed. We took an Uber to the event, and I was fine. When we were returning to our destination, we had a different Uber driver and car. The car did not have any air conditioning. I was sitting in the back of this very small car, feeling confined and uncomfortable. "I feel overheated, I need to get out of the car, can you stop the car PLEASE!" I was feeling claustrophobic. "Oh my God! Are you okay?" Shaneese asked in a caring voice. I began sweating, my heart was beating fast, and I felt like I needed to escape! I had the Uber driver stop the car, and I got out for fresh air. "Are you okay?" Carlo asked loudly. "You do not look good!" Ebony screamed. "I am okay, I just needed a little air. I did not eat breakfast this morning." I made up an excuse so that they would stop asking me questions. I was able to get back in the car, and I sat in the front seat until we reached our destination. I was extremely embarrassed about this situation. My anxiety was now front and center. People could see that something was wrong!

Anxiety attack

One night, I had an anxiety attack in my apartment, which was unusual. I had never had an attack just lying in my bed. I was awoken from my sleep by my anxiety on a Friday night. I was shaking and sweating profusely. It felt like I had caffeine jitters. The only thing I had been drinking consistently was crystal light. I was pacing in my apartment. I was freaking out! I knew it was an anxiety attack, but I had never had one at home. I had to calm myself down, but it was hard to do. I had to figure out what the trigger was for my anxiety.

Caffeine increases anxiety

I ran to the kitchen cabinets and read the label on the Crystal Light package. This flavored drink contained 10 mg of caffeine per serving. I drank a lot of it during the week. I must admit, I was beginning to feel afraid because it seemed like this anxiety thing was taking over every aspect of my life. It was triggered by the food I ate, the drinks I consumed, and numerous other things. I could not ignore this "thing" my body was doing any longer.

Anxiety appearing everywhere

The problem is that my anxious feelings began to appear more often than just in stressful situations, which is an example of Generalized Anxiety Disorder (GAD). Generalized Anxiety Disorder (GAD) is persistent and excessive worry about many things like finances, potential disasters, work, and many other issues even when there is nothing to worry about (27). An example of anxiety is avoiding elevators because you are constantly afraid or worried that you will be stuck in the elevator.

The Brockington Stages of Anxiety

My life was in turmoil. I had so much unprocessed trauma that my anxiety levels were incredibly high. My theory is the more negative life events I experienced, the more anxiety I had. I was not born with any congenital disabilities, and I had not experienced any child abuse when

I was born; my trauma happened later in my childhood. I was in the Clean Slate Stage. If I had remained in the Clean Slate Stage through adulthood, I probably would not have experienced high anxiety levels. I experienced many negative life events in adolescence and adulthood, which would explain why my anxiety was especially high.

The Brockington stages of anxiety: My theory is the more trauma you experience, the higher the potential to experience anxiety if it is not processed! **The Clean Slate Stage** is when an individual is born (baby) and has not shared any trauma or congenital disabilities. Therefore, they will probably only experience normal anxiety in their lives. For example, I was born a happy baby to a great family. There was no trauma until I was a toddler. If the baby is born with some type of trauma, they will move into the Trauma Slate Stage.

The stage where anxiety becomes problematic is the **Trauma Slate Stage**. If you were a baby, toddler, preschooler, child, adolescent, or adult and you experienced a traumatic event, and it was not processed by a professional, you will probably experience higher anxiety levels throughout your life. These individuals would then move into the **Anxiety Possibility Stage**, which consists of the six types of anxieties (phobias, generalized anxiety, panic disorder, social anxiety disorder, obsessive-compulsive disorder/post-traumatic stress disorder, or separation anxiety disorder). As you know, I suffered burn trauma as a toddler, and it has impacted my entire life. If these anxieties are processed with a professional, the individual learns to cope with the anxiety. If no traumatic experiences happened at all as a baby, toddler, preschooler, child, adolescent, or adult, then you probably would only experience normal anxiety. (Table 1.)

Clean Slate (newborn) Baby (0-12 months)	Trauma Slate Baby (0-12 months), toddler (1-3 years), preschool (3-5 years), child (5-12 years), adolescent (12-18 years), adulthood (18 and up)	Anxiety Possibility Stage
• No traumatic experiences in life • No congenital disabilities • No child abuse	One or more traumatic experiences have happened. If no trauma has occurred, the	• phobias • generalized anxiety • panic disorder • social anxiety disorder

	individual will experience normal anxiety.	• obsessive-compulsive disorder and post-traumatic stress disorder • separation anxiety disorder
If you experience trauma as a newborn, you are born into the trauma slate stage.	Unprocessed trauma is linked to higher levels of Anxiety. If processed, the individual learns to cope with the anxiety.	

Table 1.

Sandra, My Niece

Sandra is a Black girl who experienced depression and anxiety early in her life. In 1983, Sandra's mother died (**Trauma Slate Stage**). Sandra was a toddler at the time, and she did not understand the concept of death. Sandra knew that her mother was not coming back but did not understand why or if she was the cause of her mother's disappearance. Sandra's dad and two sisters moved on with life, but Sandra continued to struggle with the loss and anxiety. Sandra's dad dated different women after a year had passed, but there was one lady, Tina, who stuck around for a while.

Verbal abuse

According to Sandra, Tina did not like her or her siblings, and they disliked her as well. Long story short, Tina abused Sandra verbally. After three months, Sandra's maternal grandmother found out and decided to take Sandra and her sisters out of this situation. Sandra's father did not do well after his children left. He took a backseat in their lives, and Sandra resented him for his disappearance. Sandra lived with her grandmother until she turned 18, but she continued to struggle with the loss of her mother and worrying about her family life. There was a void extremely present in Sandra's life.

Depression and anxiety

The impact of these traumatic experiences caused Sandra to experience depression and generalized anxiety. It greatly impacted her relationship with others. She was always worrying about things where there was not a real concern. She resented her father for not keeping her safe and allowing a stranger to verbally abuse her. At age 25, Sandra struggled to have a relationship with family members and friends; she often isolated herself. At age 35, Sandra is currently seeing a therapist to process her anxiety. Sandra stated that she finds many people do not understand her pain, and they sometimes tell her to "get over it" and "depression and anxiety are not real."

Therapy

Even though Sandra participated in therapy, it was not until much later in life. Sandra struggled because her family and friends around her expected her to bounce back from her mother's death. When Sandra did not bounce back, her family members felt like something was wrong with her. The problem with Sandra's story is that she did not receive mental health therapy when the trauma happened, but once she received it, she could cope better with her anxiety. Promotion, prevention, and early intervention strategies are the best strategies for better mental health and well-being.

Jr., My Nephew

Jr. was five years old (preschool: 3-5 years) when his dad died of cancer. He and his mother maintained a very close relationship after the loss, but they both struggled with the void of not having a father or husband around. Jr.'s mother remarried, and everything seemed to be okay from his mother's perspective, but Jr. struggled with the void. Jr. would make statements like, "No one cares about me." Jr. kept to himself and would never share his emotions with anyone. In everyone's eyes, Jr. should just move on with his life; after all, his dad died years ago.

Struggling with life

Jr. was struggling with school and getting into trouble with the police. Jr. would go missing for days without letting the family know where he was. Jr. was always worried about other family members dying, and it was impacting his functioning. Jr.'s family did not provide him with the support he needed to process his grief. Most Black families, like Jr.'s, do not think their children need therapy. Jr.'s family did not see the correlation between the grief Jr. experienced and his negative behavior.

Feelings of isolation. Even though many friends and family members were around, Jr. felt alone. Jr. continued to feel lonely and sad. Jr. never sought mental health therapy. He always felt like he was not okay because he continued to feel lonely, abandoned, depressed, and anxious. Jr. was avoiding his mental health. Jr. thought that people who experience a loss should just move on. *"Time will heal all wounds."*

Identifying Sandra and Jr.'s trauma

The traumatic events Sandra experienced were her mother dying and a feeling of abandonment by her father. Jr.'s traumatic life event was his father dying. Sandra and Jr. did not recognize that the negative life experiences they went through during their childhood were trauma, and if not properly dealt with, would lead to mental health issues later in life. They both moved on with their lives and secretly suffered due to the loss of their parents.

Avoidance

Sandra and Jr. unconsciously avoided their issues. They were taught that if you have a negative situation, you just pray about it and move on. They never discussed how they felt about the situation with anyone. Black individuals are unconsciously taught to handle death and trauma by ignoring their emotions. You grieve and pray, and you expect each day to get better and better. But this does not always happen.

Trying to Find A Therapist

I was scared to seek help

I had to consider my pride

But I was afraid to be vulnerable

And put my pride aside

I need professional help

To guide me through

This journey of life

Was really forcing me to

To seek Help!

Dr. Frederick Brockington

Chapter 8: Searching For A Mental Health Professional

What I have learned so far

I have spent countless hours self-reflecting on my life and my family. I concluded that my past trauma had created my anxious behavior. The anxious behaviors I have experienced, I have also noticed in my family members. Remember, my family, experienced some of the same negative life events that I did. In the next chapter, I review the events of my life again, but from a different lens and perspective. I have more insight into my traumatic experiences. The Brockington Stages of Anxiety explains this behavior.

Everything happens for a reason

I believe that everything in life happens for a reason, and it is our job to try to understand what those reasons are. In my self-reflection, I understood where my life went off track and how it stayed off track from a mental health perspective.

After all of the negative past trauma experiences and current panic attacks, I knew I could not handle what was going on with my mental health alone. This was getting to be too much. I googled different mental health therapists in my area. I would look at their pictures and say to myself, *"Nope, I cannot go to him because he would judge me,"* or, *"I cannot go to her because she would think I was crazy."* With my mental health training, I knew I had the power to select the therapist I felt comfortable with and the therapist I felt could help me the most. I was confused about who or what I was looking for because, at this point, I had already self-diagnosed myself with anxiety. I didn't know for sure if anxiety was what I truly had. The search went on for weeks because I would constantly talk myself out of contacting a mental health professional. All the fears of being labeled with a mental illness were present and ruminating. I ultimately decided on a psychiatrist because they could prescribe medication, and I thought a psychiatrist was who I needed.

A Caucasian therapist

I finally decided on a Caucasian female psychiatrist. The reason was that I felt like a Black male therapist would judge me. This line of thinking came from my childhood and the verbal abuse experienced by my brother, a Black male. I didn't want a Black female therapist because I immediately thought of the church mothers and how they would disapprove of me not praying about this but seeking help from a secular source.

Creflo Dollar

The other day, I listened to Creflo Dollar ministries discussing depression and mental health issues. He is a Black preacher of a large church, and he has a big following. He said that church people should rely on God to help them recover from their depression. He said that everyone is running out to seek therapy, but the healing is in God. I understand what he is saying, to a point, but I feel like this type of preaching could genuinely harm people who are severely depressed or suffer from mental health issues. I chose the Caucasian female therapist for a multitude of reasons.

My fear of being vulnerable

After I set the first appointment, I felt a little relieved and scared at the same time. I had finally taken a step in the right direction to address a lifelong problem I had been experiencing. Still, I feared being vulnerable about the issues that I didn't understand myself to a total stranger of a different race. I remember thinking, *"Will she understand me? Will the cultural differences create ambiguity about my issues?"*

My appointment

I drove to my appointment on Monday, December 6th. That was an excruciatingly long drive. I had so many thoughts of turning around and keeping this problem to myself. I kept going. I pulled into the parking lot of a two-story office building. My anxiety was high as I got out of the car. I entered the building and went into suite 200. I told the receptionist that I had a 10 a.m. appointment. She asked for my insurance information and other demographics and told me to have a seat, and the doctor would see me shortly.

Uncomfortable questions

I was here and extremely anxious! The doctor called me into her office. She was very welcoming and asked me to take a seat. She asked me questions regarding myself and my family's mental health history. She asked me about my childhood, my relationship with my parents, and my siblings. She asked me if I had a lot of friends. She asked me if I had experienced any major negative life events. I was surprised because once I started talking, I told her everything I had been holding in. It was a freeing experience. I didn't know this lady, but I wanted to ensure she had all the information she needed. I told her that I thought the anxiety episode was due to consuming too much caffeine. I told her that I felt like I needed something to decrease anxiety.

Medication prescribed

She agreed that I had anxiety due to all the trauma I had experienced. She told me that she was glad I allowed her into my personal life. She thought I only needed medication when I felt claustrophobic or was experiencing a panic attack. In the session, my psychiatrist explored the different types of anxiety medication out there. She prescribed me 5mg tablets of Buspirone to be taken when needed.

Different Types of Medications to Treat Anxiety

I struggled with taking medication. I didn't want to take something I felt could change my mood or mindset. My physician assured me that the medication was tested and researched and is proven to help regulate anxiety. I decided to research some of the common medications for mental health issues. There are several different types of medications prescribed to treat anxiety. According to Harvard Health Publishing (24), common treatments of anxiety disorder are:

Drug therapy

- Antidepressants
- Benzodiazepines
- Buspirone
- Tricyclics
- MAOIs
- Beta-blockers

The serotonin reuptake inhibitors (SSRI), which are antidepressants like escitalopram (Lexapro), fluoxetine (Prozac), paroxetine (Paxil), and sertraline (Zoloft), are for long-term usage. They increase the serotonin in your brain to make you feel good.

Benzodiazepines are for short-term use, which relaxes your muscles and keeps you calm. Buspirone treats short-term and chronic anxiety disorders. Tricyclics are older drugs that treat most anxiety disorders. Monoamine oxidase inhibitors (MAOIs) treat panic disorders and social phobia. Beta-blockers block the effects of norepinephrine, which is a stress hormone that functions during the fight or flight responses. I researched this information so that I would be informed about what I was putting into my body and why.

A weight lifted off my shoulders. After speaking with my therapist/psychiatrist, I felt better. I wish I had sought treatment sooner. I am glad I didn't allow my anxiety to keep me from receiving the help I needed. She let me know that this was not my fault and with medication, I could decrease the panic attacks I was experiencing and live life again. I hope that sharing my mental health journey will help others in the Black community and all communities.

Black Boy Processing

I learned how to handle my problems at an early age.

I cried, avoided, hated, and made sure to forget the pain.

I didn't know as I got older, the memories of my younger days

Would come back to haunt me in anxious and depressing ways.

No one in my past is to blame. We are all just trying to make it

In a world full of pain.

They only did the things that helped them live.

I am learning as I get older, I must forgive.

By Dr. Frederick Dare Brockington

Chapter 9: Processing My Life Trauma Story

The scars had no pain

None of my scars physically hurt, but they created emotional anxiety. Now, in my mind, the scars are a part of me, so I certainly do not think about them often until a situation arises when the scars could potentially be exposed. For example, women, imagine gaining weight, and you already have your custom wedding dress completed. On the day of your wedding, you realize that the dress does not fit, and you have no choice but to wear the dress. As you are going down the aisle, anxiety takes over. Ruminating thoughts of how you look and what people are saying about you in the dress negatively impact your wedding day. The previous example is how I feel when faced with a situation where my burns could be exposed.

Men, imagine meeting the lady, or man, of your dreams but with the knowledge that you have a large scar hidden under your clothes when it is time to have sexual intercourse. You become anxious about being intimate with this person because you must explain the scar. You worry that you will be rejected due to the scar. Ruminating thoughts tell you not to get into this situation because you will be ashamed. You decide to stay single due to the anxiety surrounding this situation. This is how my life was when I was faced with revealing my scars. However, I now view my burn scars as badges I should be proud of and not ashamed of.

A badge of survival

I have forgiven myself for allowing the burns to control my life and create high anxiety levels. I have chosen to wear these scars and decrease my negative self-talk about them. I am processing my trauma. I have decided to take ownership of my body by exploring the scars and giving each of them meaning. I believe that when you become aware of a problem, you can begin to change the way you think about the problem. On my neck, there is a faint dark line from under my chin to my chest. This line indicates the path that the hot boiling water fell, from my head to my neck, then to my chest. For me, this specific scar symbolizes a badge of survival. I survived a life-threatening event, and I am alive to share this story.

Badge of the heart

In the center of my chest, the tissue is disfigured, and the placement of this scar prevents me from wearing an open shirt without people staring. There was a puddle of hot boiling water sitting on my chest to create this deep scar. This scar is sitting in the middle of my chest over my heart. This scar represents a badge of the heart. The trauma from the burn accident was trying to cover up the love that I should have in my heart for myself. I realize now that I can love myself, scars and all. If my partner does not love my scars, then they do not love me.

Badge of acknowledgment

On my left arm, there is a scar that is slightly visible, from the top of my left hand to the center of my arm. A splash of water created this scar during the burn experience. This scar is on my non-dominate hand, so I do not use my left hand to initiate daily activities or important things. I am right-handed, so the left hand follows what the right does. This scar symbolizes that even though I have had burn trauma, it should not dictate my life; it is a badge of acknowledgment to let myself know that I can do all things because I did survive but to not forget it. I acknowledge that I can be handsome and successful with my scars.

Purpose of the scars

The scars remain a reminder that I survived something that has unfortunately killed other people. I have a purpose in life that is attached to these scars. The scars make me unique. Yes, people will stare at the scars and make faces. In the past, this would have made me want to run and hide. I am a stronger person now. I have accepted that my scars are my story. I do not have to avoid the topic. I didn't do anything wrong. People will have to accept me for who I am. I can use my scars and my experience to help other burn victims process and share their stories.

Figuring out what to do with these burns

I was left to figure out this new life with the scars all by myself. My parents did the best they could by taking care of me after the burn trauma happened. They loved me through those difficult times. But as a child, I could not truly express my feelings every time someone looked at me weirdly. I made the best out of the situation by moving forward and creating a narrative that would explain my story during this time. I love my life. I have processed the burn trauma; now on to the next traumatic experience that needs to be processed.

The brother who liked to fight

To my brother Roy, who created abusive verbal trauma in my life, I had to forgive you for the verbal abuse you subjected to our family and me during this time. I often wonder what you were experiencing in your life that made you so bitter.

My brother was probably suffering from a type of mental illness, substance abuse addiction, or carrying some hostility for something that happened to him in the family. I often wonder what was going through his mind during those times. Did he resent me because I was the youngest child?

Did something happen in the family that created this negative person?

Disappeared from the family

Currently, Roy has isolated himself from the family. He does not come to family events. Every time I go to Virginia, I search for him, but I can never find him. I have not had any contact with him in over 20 years. I want to see him and tell him that I love him. I do not think his goal was to hurt our family or me. I am not sure what the issue was, but I have resolved it in my mind by accepting the fact that there was something else he was dealing with, and I just happened to be the target of his emotional rage. I genuinely feel sorry for him because he needed help, and no one recognized it or provided him with the treatment he deserved.

The family trait of alcohol abuse

My dad abused alcohol when I was younger. As a kid, I remember spending time with my dad during the weekends, but he would not be around due to his drinking. He would hang out with his friends, and he would come home on Sunday. He was always ready for work on Monday. I remember one Saturday, my dad was home during the weekend, and he was drunk. He was vomiting everywhere, and I didn't understand what I saw. He was closed off in his room so that he could drink in peace. My mother would always convince him that he needed to stop drinking, spend more time with his family, and start going to church. He was stubborn and did his own thing. I am not sure what happened, but suddenly, the drinking ceased.

Dad gave up alcohol

He gave up drinking alcohol after approximately 10 years and started attending church, and he changed his life completely. My dad gave his life to Christ. He became a deacon at the church. He stopped hanging out with his friends on the weekends and devoted his time to his family. He was, and still is, my hero. He used to take me to wrestling matches, and he made sure I had a car to drive in high school. Our family and I forgave his past mistakes.

Impact of dad's alcohol abuse on my brothers

The excessive drinking did not impact me as much as it probably impacted my older siblings, including my verbally abusive brother. I realized that many of my brothers had substance abuse problems due to my father's drinking problem. My dad was a great man, but in his early days, he was a heavy drinker. I remember that he would make sure all the bills were paid, and then he would disappear on the weekends.

I often wonder how my family's life was before I was born. Did something happen that was traumatic? Was my dad abusive to my mother due to his drinking? I believe all behavior is learned. Did my brother learn this verbally abusive behavior from my father? I do not have any memory of this, and my questioning of this is how I'm processing my brother's behavior.

My behavior around my brother

I have noticed that when I am around any of my brothers, I am a little timid because of all my experiences with Roy growing up. A few years ago, we had a family get-together. Everyone was having fun, playing games, grilling food, and participating in various family activities. I was playing with my nephews, just enjoying my family, and then my brother arrived. I started to get anxious, stopped playing with my nephews, and began to help grill to pull myself away from the family. I am not sure what happened to my body, but I often feel like I am hiding so that I will not be picked on. I have been working on changing this behavior now that I am aware I do this. It has gotten better. I have let go and have forgiven my brother for the verbal abuse. Processing the root of my brother's behavior and my response to his behavior has been therapeutic. No one is to blame; we are all human, and we do the best we can with what we have. Not a single one of us humans is perfect.

Church perfectionism and anxiety

Processing my relationship with the church, I realized that my church experiences were negative, despite the rules to create perfectionism. One Sunday morning, I remember being in the choir room with my church friends. We were putting on our choir robes preparing for the Sunday morning service. I was excited because I was doing a solo lead of my favorite song, "Jesus Is Real" by John P. King. The congregation loved it. Everyone was on their feet singing and clapping. I was on top of the world. I loved singing in the church choir. Not every church experience was negative.

Church made me who I am

We spent a lot of time at church, and I learned a lot. I have realized that I would not be the person I am today if I didn't grow up in the church. I learned how to love people, even if they did me wrong. I learned how to obey rules within society and how to love a group of people outside of my family. I learned that a higher being (God) protects me and guides me through life. I learned how to pray to the higher being. God was and always will be my protector and my provider. I am not blaming God for how church rules were set up.

A law-abiding citizen

I believe that my church upbringing helped me survive in the racist society I live in as a Black male. I make behavioral decisions based on my church and family upbringing. I do not steal; I respect authority, I believe no race is better than the other, so I do not look for approval from any other race. I love being a Black male, and I would not change this experience for anything. On the other hand, the church environment was not always positive.

Judgment-free zone

I realize that the church should be a judgment-free zone. When an individual is being judged, it can increase their anxiety. I realize people might not be able to abide by all the rules because of economics, mental health issues, how they were raised, and the list could go on and on. Some church members do not understand that people come to church to feel loved and often for some type of therapy. I do not think church members deliberately seek to hurt people. I think we are taught if a person does not follow the "will of God," they should be judged. The "will of God" is usually what church members utilize to judge others. I gained a lot of positive insight from my church experiences. I must give God and my church family credit.

Processing the deaths of my loved ones

To process the deaths of my family members and friends, I utilized a lot of self-reflection. Recently, I pulled out the obituaries, and I began to cry as I reviewed the date, the time, and the location of the services. The memories flooded my mind. At the time, I was not mindful of my emotions when these deaths took place. I was living my life on autopilot. I remember sitting outside of my dad's hospital room doing college homework. Getting homework done and staying busy were my ways of coping with the situation. I realize death is a part of life, and everyone will experience it. I did undergo a grieving process, but at that time, I didn't identify it as grieving. I thought I was losing my mind, honestly.

Chapter 10: The Five Stages of Grief

The Kubler-Ross model identifies the five stages of grief as denial, anger, bargaining, depression, and acceptance. I have experienced all of these during my grieving process. I didn't recognize my feelings at the time. I will describe how these stages impacted my grief-stricken process as much as I can remember so that you can understand the feelings any loss can bring. I want to normalize grief.

Denial

I was truly in denial when my family members died. I didn't want to believe it. I remember talking to my dad in the hospital, and it seemed like five minutes later, they were telling me he had died. In my mind, this just could not happen. There had to have been a mistake, or the hospital had to have done something to him. As for my mother and sister remember not believing it because I was in another state when they died. The mind is incredibly powerful. I would visit Virginia after they died and still expect to see them. I would often visit the gravesite to talk to them. I experienced this with all the deaths of my family members and friends. The next stage is anger.

Anger

Anger is an easy emotion. Anger naturally happens to everyone. I was exceptionally angry with God. I thought, *"How could the people who praised God all their lives be taken away?"* At that moment, I didn't understand the rationale behind the church, religion, and death. I think I disconnected from the church for a while because I didn't understand this phenomenon, and I punished God. I was overly angry, hurt, and sad. It does not matter if you go to church every day of your life or not; the end will inevitably always come. The next stage is bargaining.

Bargaining

When my mother, father, sister, sister-in-law, and brother-in-law were each dying, I remember praying to God, saying things like, *"If you save them, I will be more faithful in church, I will be the best person I can be, I will help others,"* and the list goes on and on. I remember as a child that I always feared my mother would die. Every hospital visit, every doctor's visit, and every sickness she experienced, I lived in fear during these moments. I was very anxious regarding the death of my parents. I would say anything to God so he would let them all live. My parents died, and I was so hurt, I didn't remember any of the promises I made to God. I was going through life on autopilot. My emotions were all over the place. After I processed these deaths as an adult, I realized the cycle of life is to be born and to die. The next stage of the grieving process is depression.

Depression

After my loved ones died, I was extremely depressed. I didn't have a desire to participate in activities as I had in the past that once gave me joy. I walked around with a chip on my shoulder after my parents died. I was not going to take any mess from anyone. I was still angry. My friends noticed an adverse change in my behavior. I was not the happy-go-lucky guy I used to be. I didn't want to hang out with them. I spent a lot of time alone. I was moody. I would cry anytime a movie had a death scene in it. I would think about family members dying all the time. My environment was tremendously dark. I felt blah! I was lost and did not know what to do. It took me years to finally accept the fact that my loved ones were deceased. The journey to acceptance of death varies in length for everyone.

Acceptance

The last stage of grief is acceptance. I finally accepted that I would not see my father, mother, sister, sister-in-law, brother-in-law, friends, and church friends here on earth ever again. This does not mean the relationship with them is over. I can keep the relationship alive by remembering them. The acceptance stage is not an easy stage to achieve. I experienced plenty of tears, mood changes, sadness, loss, and loneliness during this process. Things are better now, but I still have moments when I really miss my family members and friends. They will forever be in my heart. I moved on with my life as normally as I possibly could.

Mental Health in the Black Community

Now that I have processed my journey

It's time for me to explore

What causes my community

To simply ignore

The mental health illness that is at our doors

By Dr. Frederick Dare Brockington

Black Boys and Girls You are Not a Doctor

You did not go to medical school

Please stop being a fool

Your mental health is changing

Stop putting on a facade to look cool

The symptoms that you are experiencing

Are only going to get worse

Please seek help from a professional

So that you can always be your best

By Dr. Frederick Dare Brockington

Chapter 11: Mental Health Therapy Techniques

Therapy goals are established by the client, and as a therapist, my goal is to understand what is causing their anxiety. I explore their lives for any life events that may have triggered an anxiety response. My goal is to change their behavior patterns with cognitive behavior therapy (CBT). Most people beat themselves up with negative ruminating self-talk about what happened to them, meaning everything they think about themselves and their experiences is negative and their fault. If you read this book, you will see that I was very hard on myself throughout most of the experiences I discussed. I discussed avoiding things to survive. Life does not come with a handbook on how to handle life situations. I realized I was only doing the best I knew how. We all do the best we can to survive. It took me a long time to learn this lesson.

Do not self-diagnose

The word *diagnosis* is the act of identifying a disease, so when someone is diagnosed, a professional has decided that person meets the criteria for a specific mental health issue. As a therapist, I always tell my clients that we all have a little bit of each mental health issue, but it becomes a problem when the issue impacts our functioning. I tell my clients that they should not self-diagnose themselves. Don't give

121

yourself a mental health illness based on assumptions. I have had many clients come into the office and tell me they have a specific mental health issue because of what they read on the internet. But you cannot diagnose yourself if you are not a trained mental health professional.

When you self-diagnose, you are avoiding what is going on with you and your mental health. Intolerance of uncertainty is a mindset in which uncertainty is viewed as so concerning and aversive it must be avoided. The thing(s) you avoid will eventually come back to haunt you in your life.

CBT Therapy

A common treatment for anxiety is Cognitive Behavioral Therapy (CBT). CBT aims to provide clients with a skill that assists them in changing negative behavior and emotions due to a negative life event. Cognitive Behavioral Therapy is a form of psychological treatment that has been proven to be effective in treating various mental health issues. This book focuses specifically on anxiety. There are three core principles of CBT:

1. Most problems are based on faulty negative thinking.
2. Learned behavior patterns are created by problem-solving skills developed in the past but do not currently fit to solve the problems of the person today.
3. Individuals who are suffering can learn new behaviors, change their thinking, and live valuable lives.

An example of a treatment modality used in CBT is journaling. Ullrich and Lutgendorf (2002) believe that journaling about trauma and any triggers or stressors in one's life improves mental and physical health. Journaling is very beneficial when you need to get thoughts, feelings, and ideas out of your head and heart. When I was writing this book, I had to think of the details of my life while writing them down. This allowed me to explore my feelings and emotions about the situations I had experienced throughout my life and do some self-reflection. Journaling allows me to process anything unresolved in my life. Many CBT skills can be utilized to address changing your cognition and improving your anxiety. There are many treatments out there to assist with anxiety. Please seek a professional if you would like to know more treatment options.

Tools to Forgive Yourself

Process the situation and your role in it. Below is a step-by-step guide you can use to begin processing your traumatic event. There is no time limit in completing each step. Take the amount of time you need to process the situation, and you will know when you have completed the process.

1. Think about the situation and your role in the situation. (What happened? How was it handled? How did it change your life?)

2. What feelings were you left with once it was over?

3. What behaviors did you learn about or take away from the situation? (shut down, cry, communicate, hate men, hate women, hate yourself, guarded, etc.)
4. Are you using these behaviors in your life currently?
5. Become aware of these behaviors and try to correct them.
6. Forgive yourself for blaming yourself.

It is not your fault. Life happens to all of us, and we have to move on, but we must process what we have been through.

Progressive Muscle Relaxation

In my master's program, we learned about different cognitive-behavioral techniques. Progressive muscle relaxation (PMR) is a deep relaxation technique used to control anxiety, first introduced by Edmund Jacobson in the 1930s. I had never used it for myself, but I remembered it when I had my panic attack. Out of my toolbox, I pulled *muscle progression* and *meditation*. I used muscle progression to control the anxiety and jitters I was experiencing that Friday night. Muscle progression, in my definition, is the act of taking control of your body when it is in distress. You contract your muscles as tight as you can, starting with your feet and ending with your head. First, I would squeeze my toes together for a few seconds, as tight as I could, and then release them.

I would repeat this behavior a few times before moving on to the next muscle. Then, I would squeeze my legs together and hold that position for a few seconds, and I would also repeat this a few times. After that, I would squeeze my glutes (butt) together while sucking in my stomach for a few seconds, then squeeze my arms together in a hugging position and then release, then squeeze my eyes shut for a few seconds and repeat. The same type of muscle contraction would be repeated for my fingers, jaws, and face. This method undoubtedly helped me calm down during this period. I was able to feel more relaxed after I repeated this exercise several times. Try this method the next time you feel out of control with your anxiety. I continued to attempt to ground myself, so I decided to try a little meditation, which I also learned the importance of in my graduate program.

Meditation

The French philosopher Michel de Montaigne is quoted as having once said, *"The greatest thing in the world is to know how to belong to oneself."* Meditation will help clear the mind of all the clutter that has been accumulated. Mediation can calm you down. I wanted to understand myself and what was going on within me. During the meditation, I played some relaxing music with wave sounds, closed my eyes, and imagined I was on a beach with no anxiety or worries about what was going on in the world. Or the fact that I had been in my apartment for months without human contact. I finally was grounded and went to sleep. I still had questions, though.

You Cannot Do This by Yourself

You are not alone!

Don't keep it to yourself.

Someone is always available to listen to your stuff.

Please don't hold it in!

You will explode!

Find yourself a support system

So, you can unload your stuff!

Support Systems

A support system is when you have an individual or a group of people you can confide in about your problems. Social Support (SS) is defined as the emotional support individuals receive from family, friends, and support groups. To reduce mental health disorders, social support has been a proven method. You can tell your support system anything, and they will listen and give you their perspective. The SS can also provide you with resources to help solve your issues. A support system could be a brother, sister, best friend, teacher, counselor, grandmother, etc. I went through my childhood accepting the verbal abuse from my brother without talking to my parents about it. I am not entirely sure why I didn't tell anyone how I was feeling. My parents would have talked with my brother so that he would have treated me better. I genuinely wish I had the skillset back then to tell them how I felt about the family situation.

I would likely not be as anxious today if I had resolved this situation during my childhood. I remember as a child I was rather daring. I loved to sing in front of people. When I was 7 years old at Wythe Elementary School, I entered a talent show. I had a lot of neighborhood friends who certainly made my childhood fun. We would play kickball in the local field. I didn't have a care in the world. I genuinely enjoyed being in front of people until I got old enough to understand that I had flaws. I feel like I lost my creativity as a child after my brother consistently harassed me. I feel like my life would have been so different if I had spoken to my support system. My family was great, but every family has flaws and areas for growth. When I was a child, I didn't know what a support system was. I beg you, Black girls and boys, please have a conversation with your family, especially your children, about support systems.

Hard Conversations about Mental Health Issues

Please have hard conversations with family members or friends if you are struggling with functioning mentally in your daily life due to trauma or a negative life event. To start a conversation, you need to understand yourself and your emotions related to the traumatic situation. Here is how to address the conversation.

- **Sit with your emotions regarding the situation:** Ask yourself the following questions: What emotions am I feeling? What is my primary emotion regarding the situation? How did the situation impact my life and my relationships with others? Identify any triggers for the situation. Establish this step before moving to the next step.

- **Now that you understand the impact and emotions as it relates to the situation in your life, you must carefully confront others, if necessary:** Provide eye contact! Take ownership of your part, but others must also take ownership of theirs. With love and kindness, confront these individuals using *"I"* statements. *I* felt this, *I* did that, etc. You can now continue to the next step.

- **Schedule a conversation with the individual or individuals:** Discuss what your life has been like after the situation. (Again, use *"I"* statements.) *I have experienced a hard life due to [fill in the blank].* Discuss your feelings, your emotions, and how you would like to move past the situation. Allow the other person time to talk! Do not interrupt them. If emotions run high, take a break, but revisit the conversation when both individuals are calm. This may take extra time, or the person may no longer be interested in completing the conversation at all. The good thing is that you have processed the event yourself in step one.

- **Close the chapter:** Once you feel like you have processed all your emotions with yourself and everyone involved, you can move forward. At this point, you should understand your triggers regarding the situation.

- **Mindfulness:** You must be mindful of your triggers! When those emotions related to the past event present themselves in your current life after you have closed the chapter recognize them, sit with them, and move forward.

It is okay to ask questions. I hope that everyone finds an individual or family therapist who they can trust with their mental health. When searching for a therapist, make sure to decide if you want them to be male or female, Black, White, or another race, licensed or unlicensed, etc. You have the right to select a therapist that you feel comfortable with. You should feel like you can be completely vulnerable with this person. If you have any negative feelings about them, you can find a new therapist. Ultimately, you are the customer. Remember to treat your mental health like you would your physical health. They are both incredibly important.

I Apologize, Mental Health

I Apologize for Mental Health.

I have not always treated you the best.

I was taught to take care of the physical,

Forsaking my mental health was so detrimental.

If I could do it all again,

I would treat my mental health like my best friend.

I am not broken

Kanye West, a famous rapper in the United States, has been acting strange. He became friends with Donald Trump, and the Black community did not like it. He attempted to run for president and showed bizarre behaviors over the last few years. The Black community believes Kanye West is "crazy." Kanye was diagnosed with bipolar disorder in 2016. Kanye West's wife, Kim Kardashian, recently filed for divorce. Kanye is not "broken," he has a mental health issue and needs help. He felt the pressure against him from the Black community, so he supported Donald Trump, who some of the Black community believed was a racist. I could see why Kanye West might have felt abandoned by his community because of his strange behavior.

I remember having thoughts of wishing I were twenty-something again because my anxiety was not so visible. At moments, I felt ashamed that I could not ride an elevator because my anxiety caused me to walk up flights of stairs instead. I am not "broken" just because I have anxiety. I feel like when people in the Black community find out that you have a mental health issue, they make you feel alone or like you have done something wrong. I do not think the Black community means to ostracize that person, but it happens subconsciously. The Black community must start looking at mental health illness as an illness and not a social disease or stigma.

I must admit that when I was younger, I viewed a person with a mental health illness as "less human." I thought that they needed to be taken away, or else I had to stay away from them so that I would not catch "it." I am glad I have learned that mental health illness is just like a physical illness. They both must be treated for the individual to get better.

Broken system for mental health

Mental illnesses are health conditions involving changes in emotions, thoughts, or behaviors, or a combination of these. We all experience changes in our emotions, thoughts, and behaviors, but that does not mean we are broken. I am not broken because I may hear voices. I am not broken because I cannot ride on an elevator due to my claustrophobia. I am not broken because I am bipolar. I am not broken because I suffer from PTSD. I am not broken because I suffer from ADHD. I am not broken because I suffer from a mental illness. I am still human! I am capable of love, and I still need love. My life matters, even if I do have a mental health illness.

This stigma not only exists in the Black community but also in the prison systems, which house many Black men. Black and African American people are over-represented in our jails and prisons and account for 40% of the prison population. The Black boys and men at a Florida prison are being abused because the system has failed them by not providing proper mental health care. The inmates have been diagnosed with various mental health issues, which trigger them to have conflicts with the correctional officers. Also, the correctional officers are not trained as mental health professionals, which is another issue. I understand that the guards get frustrated, but the inmates are human and deserve proper mental health treatment.

Dee, a 25-year-old African American male, was in a Florida prison for several years before he died. Dee was always getting in trouble with the law since he was 13 years old. Dee was diagnosed with bipolar disorder and used marijuana to calm himself down. I recently filmed a YouTube interview about this story which focused on Black boys in a mental health facility prison in Florida.

I interviewed Dee's mother and her friend, who also has a son in the same prison. The mothers reported that the staff was mistreating their sons. Dee's mother stated that her son would report the threats he received daily to her. He reported that he was locked in solitary confinement without food sometimes. He also told her about all of his negative emotions while confined due to his bipolar disorder. They were beaten, their medication withheld as punishment, and correctional officers threatened to take them home in a body bag. Denying a patient's medication will inevitably make the situation worse.

Dee eventually died in the facility, and the administration acted as if they did not know what had happened to him. His cause of death is marked as suicide. His mother believes he was beaten to death and covered up. The mother of the other inmate is still there, raising concerns about the same things Dee was. I felt bad for these inmates because I have anxiety and sometimes feel alone because, you know, people do not truly understand the issues you face unless they have gone through them, too. If it is not a physical ailment and you can't see it, most people do not understand it.

This is a significant concern for my community and me. I noticed there is a new trend in 2021 to get Black men and women seeking therapy. One of my goals is to help as many Black people understand the importance of therapy and how mental health can help increase communication among family members, help express emotions better, and handle conflict effectively.

Life has been hard for us.

I feel like the Black and Brown communities always experience higher levels of traumatic and negative life events than other races, which continues to be the case (10). A lot of us are homeless. Many of us are stuck in generational curses where our grandparents or great-grandparents have lived in poverty, and we continue the cycle and do not know how to get out of it. A lot of us are on drugs or living paycheck to paycheck—a lot of trauma on top of trauma. Currently, a movement called Black Lives Matter (BLM) is trying to highlight social concerns.

Conclusion

Black boys and Black girls, I love you! I want the best for you and our communities. I want us to love ourselves, body, mind, and spirit. The help can come in many forms like education about a topic, mentoring, love, sharing, financially, and spiritually. It's okay to have a mental health illness. We must make sure we treat our temple like the kings and queens that we are. We deserve the best!

For struggling individuals, you have to identify the internal conflicts that the anxiety is creating. What seems hard about the issue or conflict that you are experiencing? Once you have done that, you can communicate to yourself and a professional what the problem is and what you want the resolution to look like. You may not know the solution right away, but it will eventually come to you. I believe that we all have the answers to our problems, but we sometimes need a therapist to help us bring out the solution. Please consider that you will likely fight internally with yourself before you realize that you need professional help, and there is a therapist uniquely set aside to help you. You do not have to do this alone.

Therapy helps by allowing you to speak to someone else openly and confidentially about the trauma you have been holding inside. Therapists provide active listening and eye contact to feel like your voice is being heard. Therapy is challenging when you first start, but if you put the work in, the end result is worth it. My search for healing was rather long and rough. I suffered from anxiety, but I realized there was a light at the end of the tunnel.

Poems

In this section, I have written several poetry pieces that you can use to explore your emotions as it relates to your mental health. I wrote them based on some of my feelings when I was dealing with my anxious self. I hope they can help you with your self-reflection.

Healing

I am not broken; I just need help

The emotions in my head have me scared

I am afraid if I tell someone

They will look at me funny

Or they might tell my family

That I am crazy and acting weird

But I need to tell someone

So that I can get help

To deal with the anxiety

Inside myself

Heal me now, make me better

I can do this if

My load is lighter

I Cry at Night

I am scared, I am not ashamed to say

My mind has changed in a strange way

I feel that I have lost control

The things I used to do I can't do anymore

What happened to me when I was young

It was a long time ago, but it has dimmed the sun

I cry myself to sleep every night

Hope that the next day will become bright

I Can Make It

I can beat this mental illness

It is not in control

I must understand it

So that I can move on

It will not define me

Make me feel strange

I will define it

By taking control

I can make it

I know I can

I won't give up on me

I am a strong (Black) Man

Community Support

Black community, I need your help

I want to tell you that I need help

My mental health has been challenged

But with your support

I can win this battle

Life is hard; life is tough

Mental health illness

Is something we need to discuss

References

1. Egberts, M. R., van de Schoot, R., Boekelaar, A., Hendrickx, H., Geenen, R., Van Loey, N. E., & E. (2016). Child and adolescent internalizing and externalizing problems 12 months post burn: The potential role of pre burn functioning, parental posttraumatic stress, and informant bias. *European Child & Adolescent Psychiatry, 25*(7), 791-803. http://dx.doi.org/10.1007/s00787-015-0788-z

2. Bakker, A., van der Heijden, Peter G, M., van Son, M. J., , M., van de Schoot, R., E. (2014). The relationship between behavioral problems in preschool children and parental distress after a pediatric burn event. *European Child & Adolescent Psychiatry, 23*(9), 813-22. http://dx.doi.org/10.1007/s00787-014-0518-y

3. Price, M., Pallito, S., & Legrand, A. C. (2018). Heterogeneity in the strength of the relation between social support and post-trauma psychopathology. *Journal of Psychopathology and Behavioral Assessment, 40* (2), 334-343.

4. Clefberg Liberman, L., & Öst, L. (2016). The relation between fears and anxiety in children with specific phobia and parental fears and anxiety. *Journal of Child and Family Studies, 25*(2), 598-606.

5. Frank,C (2008). What is the difference between anxiety and phobia? Retrieved from https://abcnews.go.com/Health/AnxietyOverview/story?id=4659885

6. Clark, C. N., Downey, L. E., Golden, H. L., Fletcher, P. D., Rajith, d. S., Cifelli, A., & Warren, J. D. (2014). "The mind is its own place": Amelioration of claustrophobia in semantic dementia. *Behavioural Neurology, 2014*

7. Paddock, M. (2017) Medical News Today. What's to know about claustrophobia?. Retrieved from https://www.medicalnewstoday.com/articles/37062#causes

8. Silverman, W. K., & Others. (1995), What do children worry about? Worries and their relation to anxiety. In *Child Development* (Vol. 66, Issue 3, pp. 671–686).

9. Doyle, O., PhD, Joe, S., PhD, & Caldwell, C. H., PhD. (2012). Ethnic differences in mental illness and mental health service use among black fathers. *American Journal of Public Health, 102*, S222-31. Retrieved from https://www.proquest.com/docview/1017604785?accountid=36783&forcedol=true

10. Mental Health America, 2018. Retrieved from https://www.mhanational.org/issues/black-and-African-American-communities-and-mental-health

11. Puckett, J. A., Maroney, M. R., Levitt, H. M., & Horne, S. G. (2016). Relations between gender expression, minority stress, and mental health in Cisgender sexual minority women and men. *Psychology of Sexual Orientation and Gender Diversity.*

12. Robinson, M. A., Jones-Eversley, S., Moore, S. E., Ravenell, J., & Adedoyin, A. C. (2018). Black male mental health and the black church: Advancing a collaborative partnership and research agenda. *Journal of Religion and Health, 57*(3), 1095-1107. doi:http://dx.doi.org/10.1007/s10943-018-0570-x

13. Mental Health America, 2021. Retrieved from https://www.mhanational.org/racial-trauma

14. University of Liverpool. (2013, October 16). Traumatic life events biggest cause of anxiety, depression. *ScienceDaily*. Retrieved May 29, 2020, from www.sciencedaily.com/releases/2013/10/131016213223.html

15. Cruz, M., Pincus, H. A., Harman, J. S., Reynolds, C. F., & Post, E. P. (2008). Barriers to care-seeking for depressed African Americans. *International Journal of Psychiatry in Medicine, 38*(1), 71-80. Retrieved from https://search.proquest.com/docview/196305881?accountid=36783

16. Murry, V. M., Heflinger, C. A., Suiter, S. V., & Brody, G. H. (2011). Examining perceptions about mental

health care and help-seeking among rural African american families of adolescents. *Journal of Youth and Adolescence, 40*(9), 1118-31. doi:http://dx.doi.org/10.1007/s10964-010-9627-1

17. Mental Health America 2020, Retrieved from https://mhanational.org/issues/202/mental-health-america-prevalence-data

18. Blackman, T, (2018) 3 shows normalizing black mental health (and doing it well. https://themighty.com/2018/01/tv-television-shows-normalizing-mental-health-illness/

19. Banks, A, B, (2015) Black churches bucking the trend of the decline. Retrieved from: https://www.washingtonpost.com/national/religion/black-churches-bucking-the-trend-of-decline/2015/08/13/9644fa64-41f7-11e5-9f53-d1e3ddfd0cda_story.html

20. Assari S, Mistry R, Caldwell CH, Zimmerman MA. Marijuana use and depressive symptoms; Gender differences in African American adolescents. Front Psychol. 2018 Nov 16:9:2135. doi: 10.3389/fpsyg.2018.02135. PMID: 30505287; PMCID: PMC6250838.

21. Gray, C., Carter, R., & Silverman, W. (2011). Anxiety symptoms in African American children: Relations with ethnic pride, anxiety sensitivity, and parenting. *Journal*

of Child & Family Studies, 20(2), 205–213.
https://doi.org/10.1007/s10826-010-9422-3

22. *Psychology & Psychiatry Journal* (2014) findings from Harvard University broaden understanding of anxiety disorders (theory of mind impairments in social anxiety disorder). (2014, Aug 02). Retrieved from https://search.proquest.com/docview/1547901148?acco untid=36783Anxiety disorders

23. Harvard Health Publishing Harvard Medical School, Anxiety and physical illness (2018) retrieved from https://www.health.harvard.edu/category/staying-healthy

24. United Kingdom National Health Service (NHS) (2018) retrieved from https://www.nhs.uk/mental-health/conditions/generalised-anxiety-disorder/syptoms/

25. Gadye, L (2020). What part of the brain deals with anxiety? What can brains affected by anxiety tell us? Retrieved from https://www.brainfacts.org/diseases-and-disorders/mental-health/2018/what-part-of-the-brain-deals-with-anxiety-what-can-brains-affected-by-anxiety-tell-us-062918

26. Anxiety & Depression Association of America (n. D) Retrieved from https://adaa.org/understanding-anxiety/generalized-anxiety-disorder-gad#:~:text=Generalized%20Anxiety%20Disorder%20(

GAD)%20is,difficult%20to%20control%20their%20wo
rry

27. Colizzi, M., Lasalvia, A & Ruggeri, M. (2020)
Prevention and early intervention in youth mental
health: is it time for a multidisciplinary and trans-
diagnostic model for care?

28. Gregory, C. (2020) The five stages of grief: An
examination of the Kubler-ross model. Retrieved from
https://www.psycom.net/depression.central.grief.html

29. Hearn, C. S., Donovan, C. L., Spence, S. H., March, S.,
& Holmes, M. C. (2017). What's the worry with social
anxiety? Comparing cognitive processes in children
with generalized anxiety disorder and social anxiety
disorder. *Child Psychiatry and Human
Development, 48*(5), 786-795.

30. American Psychological Association, 2017 Retrieved
from: https://www.apa.org/ptsd-_guideline/patients-
and-families/cognitive-behavioral

31. Ullrich, P. M., M.A., & Lutgendorf, S. K., PhD. (2002).
Journaling about stressful events: Effects of cognitive
processing and emotional expression. *Annals of
Behavioral Medicine, 24*(3), 244-50.
doi:http://dx.doi.org/10.1207/S15324796ABM2403_10

32. WebMD. (2020). Progressive muscle relaxation for
stress an insomnia. Retrieved from:

https://www.webmd.com/sleep-disorders/muscle-relaxation-for-stress-insomnia

33. American Psychiatric Association para 1, 2021 retrieved from https://www.psychiatry.org/patients-families/what-is-mental-illness